A
HOPEFUL
HEART

⇒ *A* ⇐
HOPEFUL
HEART

Louisa May Alcott
Before LITTLE WOMEN

DEBORAH NOYES

schwartz & wade books · new york

A Note on Language

A prolific journal and letter writer, Louisa May Alcott was at times cavalier about spelling, grammar, and punctuation—and fond of lively slang or made-up words, like "perwerse." For flavor and authenticity, the author has retained Alcott's original text and formatting.

Visit us on the Web! rhcbooks.com

Educators and librarians, for a variety of teaching tools, visit us at RHTeachersLibrarians.com.

Library of Congress Cataloging-in-Publication Data
Names: Noyes, Deborah, author.
Title: A hopeful heart: Louisa May Alcott before Little Women / Deborah Noyes.
Description: First edition. | New York: Schwartz & Wade Books, [2020] |
Includes bibliographical references and index. | Audience: Ages 8–12. | Audience: Grades 7–9. |
Summary: "A middle-grade biography about literary icon Louisa May Alcott"
—Provided by publisher.
Identifiers: LCCN 2020014513 | ISBN 978-0-525-64623-5 (hardcover)
ISBN 978-0-525-64624-2 (library binding) | ISBN 978-0-525-64625-9 (ebook)
Subjects: LCSH: Alcott, Louisa May, 1832–1888—Juvenile literature. | Women authors, American—19th century—Biography—Juvenile literature.
Classification: LCC PS1018 .N69 2020 | DDC 813/.4—dc23

The text of this book is set in 12.25-point Adobe Caslon.
Book design by Rachael Cole

MANUFACTURED IN SOUTH KOREA

10 9 8 7 6 5 4 3 2 1

First Edition

For Lisa

CONTENTS

From her father she received pride, intellect, and will; from her mother passion, imagination, and the fateful melancholy of a woman defrauded of her dearest hope. . . . These two masters ruled soul and body, warring against each other.

—Louisa May Alcott, *Moods*

THE FORBIDDEN–APPLE EXPERIMENT

1832–1834

She has withstood the temptations of the appetites
through a whole morning, and though they triumphed,
at last, the triumph was not without a struggle.

—*Amos Bronson Alcott, journal, 1833*

*L*ouisa May Alcott never liked her birthday. "On a dismal November day I found myself," as she put it, and "began my long fight."

Her mother remembered that day in 1832—and her daughter—differently. The infant Louisa was a "sprightly, merry little puss," Abigail Alcott wrote, "quirking up her mouth and cooing at every sound."

Louisa the fighter found herself in the heart of an unusual family.

Amos Bronson Alcott, Louisa's father, was an educator and philosopher fascinated by human nature. Louisa's mother shared his ideals and was fiercely committed to social change.

When Anna, the first of four Alcott daughters, was born on March 16, 1831 twenty months before Louisa—Bronson wrote grandly, "A child is given. May we guide it in the paths of truth." He saw the new baby as an invitation to a great experiment: What is human happiness? Can it be built from the ground up? Can parents limit outside influences and raise a perfect child? How do children learn?

To find out, he took scrupulous notes on his firstborn's mental and moral growth. He looked and listened, like any attentive father, but also exposed Anna to stimuli, like a scientist. What faces would she make? What sounds and gestures? His laboratory was built on gentleness and reason, but Bronson's curiosity sometimes got the better of him. What would happen, for instance, if he made a scary face? (That experiment "must not be repeated," he concluded. Fear, however mild, only subtracted from a child's happiness.)

He called his journal "Observations of the Life of my First Child" and intended it to be no less than a "history of the human mind . . . faithfully narrated."

Louisa arrived in the world on Bronson's thirty-third birthday, and she too became part of the family experiment.

The sisters were in every way a study in contrasts, their father observed.

Bronson believed in the divine purity of young children: newborns came into the world still in touch with instincts and intuition from the spiritual realm. Mild, sentimental, and eager to please, Anna was fair and serene like her father. She fit his concept of the ideal infant.

Louisa, with her "vivid, energetic" power, individuality, and force, did not. An active, fretful baby, she challenged her father's theories from the beginning (and would challenge him all her life).

Louisa was practical and proud, with a fierce will, imagination, and temper. She had storm-dark eyes—some said gray, others black—and her mother's olive skin.

In a letter to his own mother, Bronson praised his wife's maternal devotion. She "lives and moves and breathes" for her family, he wrote. But at the same time, he gave Abby full credit, or blame, for the baffling phenomenon that was Louisa.

Overworked and in poor health during the formative early months of her daughter's life, even Abby looked back and blamed herself for Louisa's moodiness.

Born with "the wild exuberance of a powerful nature," Louisa was certainly "fit for the scuffle of things," as Bronson put it, and their household was nothing if not a scuffle.

Clamoring for the attention of two intellectual, socially active parents, toddler Anna lashed out at her mother and sometimes struck her. Anna slapped and scratched Louisa the intruder one minute—though she always agonized afterward—and slathered Louisa in kisses the next.

Not to be outdone, tiny Louisa mastered the art of the

tantrum, learning to howl and collapse into a heap on the floor, wedging her head between her knees and screaming bloody murder. Sobbing before bedtime became one of her "most confirmed habits."

Trying to mold the perfect family in crowded chaotic conditions wore on Bronson. The family lived at the time in Germantown, Pennsylvania—about six miles outside Philadelphia—while he tested his radical educational methods at a suburban school funded by wealthy Quakers. His roles as father and educator were hard to separate, and with his suburban experiment on the wane and bills piling up, Bronson closed the Germantown school. He rented an apartment in the city of Philadelphia, leaving Abby to manage the girls and the household alone. Bronson disappeared into the hallowed halls of Philadelphia's public library collections to study educational tracts and philosophy, and walked six miles each way on weekends to spend time in Germantown with the family.

On April 22, 1833, he opened a new school in the city with fifteen students, and while Abby and the girls occupied a series of boardinghouses in Germantown and then Philadelphia, Bronson kept his distance.

When he visited the family, he and Abby argued over responsibility. His absence kept her mind "in a state of excitement," she confessed. He was "unkind, indifferent, and improvident," and when he *was* present, he held "too closely to the ideal" of a family, leaving no room for error.

Bronson saw educational reform as both "duty and right" and argued that in order to make a difference in the world, he had to live and defend a serene life of the mind. "Sacrifices must be made to the spirit of the age," he reasoned. "My family must feel the evil of this to some degree, but this should not deter me."

Louisa and Anna continued to be subjects of their father's intellectual inquiry. One of Bronson's child-development experiments featured a shiny, forbidden apple.

He sat his daughters down one day and asked, "Should little girls take things that do not belong to them without asking their fathers or mothers—things to eat or drink—things they may like?"

"They should not," asserted four-year-old Anna.

Did the girls think that if they should see an apple, they would ever take it without asking for it?

Anna shook her head. No. Never.

Louisa agreed.

Bronson then set an apple out where the girls would see it and quit the room. At dinnertime he returned to find a browning core on the table by Louisa. Once the family finished their meal, Bronson asked about the object near her plate. What was it?

"Apple," Louisa said.

"Where did you get it?"

Her eyes darted to Anna, who could barely contain herself.

"I told her she must not," blurted the obedient older sister, "but she did!" They had both taken a few bites before Anna had thrown the apple into the fireplace grate. But Louisa had seized it and finished it. "I was naughty," Anna confessed. "I didn't ask you, as I ought to—shall you punish me father, for it?"

Bronson had put the apple there on purpose to "try" them, he explained. "I rather thought you *would* take it; but I hoped you would think of what I had said and that you *would not* take it. Did you think you were doing right?"

"No," said Anna, "my conscience told me I was not."

"And shall you mind it next time?" he asked.

"Yes, I think I shall."

"Well, Anna, always *mind* that, and then you will do right."

Louisa toddled over, and he pulled her up onto his knee. Had she eaten some of the apple?

"Yes, I did."

"Why did you take it before father said you might have it?"

She smiled ear to ear. "I wanted it."

Louisa's turn at playing Eve to her father's Jehovah didn't end there. Bronson conducted at least one other such test with her as subject, leaving an apple conveniently in sight while he hid nearby to watch.

Faced with the forbidden fruit, Louisa scolded herself: "No, no—father's—me not take father's apple—naughty!"

But her plump little hand reached out.

Louisa didn't eat the apple at first. She played with it and *nearly* ate it—*several* times, her father recorded—but in the end, temptation won, and conscience lost. "Me *must* have it," she told the air, biting into the apple's crisp flesh.

Bronson didn't punish Louisa. (He had seen his "spiritual principle" in action: his youngest had struggled with the question, and that was enough.) Though surely she felt the wages of her sin. For not the first time, Louisa had disappointed her father.

But she was not one to be daunted.

By the time she was eighteen months old, Louisa and her sister had already lived at four different addresses while their father was looking for a foothold as a teacher.

The new school struggled on for a year, though Bronson no longer saw Philadelphia as fertile ground for educational reform. The people there seemed to him material-minded, "not deeply interested in intellectual and moral subjects." In the end, this project failed like the other. The parents of Bronson's pupils continued to find his methods—such as asking children to keep diaries of their spiritual and intellectual progress—unconventional and unsettling, and pulled their children out.

Philadelphia might not be ready for an experimental classroom, Bronson supposed, but maybe Boston was.

The family had "continued at this place 2 years," Abby wrote in her journal, "with uncertain and vacillating prospects of success." They decided to return, without delay, to her home city. Over the years and decades to come, Abby would master the art and particulars of relocating her family, and once a decision was made, plans would develop quickly.

On the day of the move, Abby—"Marmee" to her girls—dressed Anna and Louisa in clean, crisp traveling frocks. The Alcotts and their belongings were not long aboard the Boston-bound steamboat when toddler Louisa wandered off, as she would throughout her childhood, in search of adventure.

A panicked search ensured, and the family found their naughty runaway, at last, belowdecks in the engine room. Louisa sat lost in play, oblivious to steam and danger and the ship's clanking machinery, her white dress smeared with soot.

RECORD

OF

CONVERSATIONS ON THE GOSPELS.

View of Mr. Alcott and the Children conversing.

CONVERSATION I.
IDEA OF SPIRIT.

EVIDENCE OF CONSCIOUSNESS.

Introduction. — Method. — Sentiment of Spirit.

I. METAPHYSICAL AND PSYCHOLOGICAL FACTS.

1. Testimony of External Senses, — Their Office; Fruits.
2. Testimony of Internal Senses, — Their Office; Intuition of Spirit; Analysis of Functions and Offices; Terms.

MR. ALCOTT. WE are now going to speak
Introduction.   of the Life of Christ. If any of you are
interested to understand how Jesus came into this
world; and lived; and acted; and went back to God;

1

≈2≈

QUEEN
OF THE
REVEL

1834-1835

My father taught in the wise way which unfolds
what lies in the child's nature, as a flower blooms,
rather than crammed it, like a Strasbourg
goose, with more than it could digest.

—*from* Louisa May Alcott: Her Life, Letters, and Journals

*B*ronson's magnetic charm with children and his radical teaching methods fast became the talk of Boston, thanks in part to family friend Elizabeth Palmer Peabody, herself a brilliant educator.

A classical scholar gifted in mathematics and languages, among other subjects, Peabody was "amazed" by the student work Bronson sent from Pennsylvania, especially the caliber of the children's writing.

His mission as an educator, Bronson told her, was to draw out, through guided conversation, ideas and truths already present in a child's mind and spirit. By asking pointed questions, he encouraged pupils to discover and decide for themselves. He would gently lead them to define a position or reach the conclusion the teacher sought—but on their own. He also maintained that children were holy innocents, with something to teach adults.

This was news to Boston—news that Peabody spread with enthusiasm, drumming up early support among the city's intellectual elite and its foremost citizens. Bronson Alcott seemed to Peabody a bright light with an unmatched "genius for education."

When enough families had committed, Bronson rented

space for his experimental school upstairs in the Masonic Temple on Boston's Tremont Street. He invited Elizabeth Peabody to assist him—without pay at first—and she accepted. The school opened its doors on September 22, 1834, with twenty students, the majority from prominent families and under age ten. Nearly half of them were girls. (Parents may have been more willing to experiment with girls' education; most girls in that era would not proceed to trades or higher learning.) The youngest pupil was a grandson of former president John Quincy Adams.

Sunlight poured through a high arched Gothic window into the spacious schoolroom. Plaster faces of Plato, Socrates, Shakespeare, and the Scottish writer Sir Walter Scott gazed down with blank eyes from pedestals in corners. Paintings lined the walls, and each tidy desk had its own private bookshelf.

Chock-full of objects to inspire thirsty minds—alarm clocks, decks of cards, a globe, an hourglass—Bronson's schoolroom even kept a pitcher of water at the ready to quench thirsty bodies. He had thought of everything, it seemed.

When the tall, blue-eyed scholar walked in that first day, addressing students in his serene voice, "Every face was eager and interested," Elizabeth Peabody reported. In her notes for that day, she wrote:

Mr. Alcott sat behind his table, and the children were placed in chairs, in a large arc around him; the chairs so far apart, that they could not easily touch each other. He then asked each one separately, what idea he or she had of the purpose of coming to school? To learn; was the first answer. To learn what? By pursuing this question, all the common exercises of school were brought up by the children themselves.

Bronson divided human personality into four major aspects: animal nature, affection, conscience, and intellect. A good teacher educated the *whole* child, including physical or "animal" needs—and so the day began with play.

After fun and games came conversation. Bronson's method of Socratic dialogue—a system of rational questioning developed by the ancient Greek philosopher Socrates, which draws out a subject's implicit knowledge—gave students the chance to share their own wisdom. They were also encouraged to sing and clap between lessons.

Bronson's methods were highly unusual at a time when most teachers viewed children as wild hooligans in need of civilizing, when instruction amounted to memorization drills, and when misconduct earned stern punishment. Many schoolmasters of the day practiced corporal punishment—smacking a child's bottom with a paddle or the knuckles with a ruler—on a routine basis to keep order in the classroom, and here again Bronson broke the mold. "The child has rights," he wrote, "as well as the adult. The right of self-government, and the liberty to govern."

He refused to punish a student until the offender acknowledged that the punishment was just.

When two boys acted out one day in class, Bronson proposed that some children might find it worse to inflict pain than to receive it. He held out his own hand and ordered the offending boys to strike him.

A "profound and deep stillness" fell over the classroom, Elizabeth Peabody recorded. The boys took their punishment, striking their teacher's hand with the ruler, but their eyes shone with tears.

Peabody came to live with the Alcotts in their boardinghouse lodgings on Chauncey Street in Boston, which was a relief for pregnant Abby. "She is very fond and sweet with children," Abby wrote, "and often keeps mine for hours interested in stories and pictures to her own evident satisfaction."

Abby also admired Peabody as a person and enjoyed her company. "She is truly good . . . very poor, but hopeful and resolute. She is not the first genius that has craved bread."

Though Anna and Louisa were not students at the Temple School—they were still deemed too young—Bronson sometimes evoked their presence in class to illustrate a moral lesson, as when he shared about one of Louisa's bouts with selfishness.

"Two little girls were standing in the parlor with their mother," he told his students, "and their father, looking over his papers, found a beautiful picture."

The father in Bronson's narrative gives the picture to the older girl, and the younger, in a fit of envy, lashes out: "I don't like father."

"I will give you a picture," the father offers, locating another, but the little girl complains. That picture isn't nearly as pretty.

The father then asks the obedient older sister if she would consider sacrificing the picture for her sibling's sake. Older sister doesn't hesitate to give the picture to her sibling. Younger hangs her head and pouts, prompting the father to ask, "Which is the best girl"—the one who gives away her picture, or the one who takes it?

"The one who gives it away," younger sister begrudges.

Bronson then described what happens when the father leaves the room.

The penitent trails after: "Father, I'm going to give this picture back again." And so the little girl does.

Whether the pupil was one of his own children or the grandson of a former president, Bronson used discussion and debate this way to guide a child to reach her own conclusions (or to reach the teacher's conclusions on her own). Education, Bronson maintained, was the art of asking "apt and fit questions."

* * *

When a third Alcott daughter was born on June 24, 1835, Bronson named the baby Elizabeth Peabody Alcott in tribute to his assistant and friend.

The new baby, nicknamed Lizzie, was a picture of serenity. Bronson started another chronicle at once, this time planning to publish his findings as "Psyche, or The Breath of Childhood." (His observations of the early childhood years of his three older daughters would eventually reach twenty-five hundred pages.)

Anna was on her best behavior with the mild newcomer, but toddler Louisa was wary. "It has a little head and pretty hair. . . . Let me take it in my arms," she said. Then she decided, "I don't love little sister. I wish she was dead. . . . I will throw her out the window."

After being punished and sent sobbing to her bed, Louisa confessed later: "I am very naughty. . . . I feel bad. Father don't love me, mother don't love me . . . little sister . . ."

Bronson soothed her with forgiveness, and so it went, a cycle of sin and redemption.

Elizabeth Peabody, who witnessed Bronson's disciplinary and educational methods firsthand—both at home and at school—

compiled her ongoing classroom reportage for publication the following July.

The much-discussed book, *Record of a School: Exemplifying the General Principles of Spiritual Culture,* made shocking observations such as "A teacher should never forget that the mind he is directing may be on a scale larger than his own." Bronson's goal, and the philosophy of the Temple School, was to teach students to think for themselves, a startling idea then, as now. In other writings, he argued that "the true teacher defends his pupils against his own personal influence. He inspires self-trust."

The curious trickled in to visit the model school, from as far away as London. The visitors sat on a plush green velvet couch in the corner to take in Bronson's experimental methods, to witness firsthand the secret workings of child development.

A swift success, the Temple School became a magnet and a salon for Boston's big intellects, including the minister William Ellery Channing, whose daughter Mary attended the school, and the writer and fellow transcendentalist who would become Bronson's closest friend, Ralph Waldo Emerson.

At the heart of transcendentalism, New England's new idealistic philosophical and social movement, was the idea that all nature, including human nature, was good and holy. Transcendentalists such as Bronson and Emerson believed that society and its institutions had corrupted the purity of the individual.

People did their best thinking outside the bounds of conformity. To be self-reliant and spontaneous in thought, trusting your own instincts and intuition, was to be in harmony with nature and the divine.

Exciting and radical views on feminism, abolition, and communal living were bubbling up around these ideas and found their way into the classroom. Elizabeth Peabody wasn't the only overqualified female employee at the Temple School during its seven years of operation. The writer Margaret Fuller (who would edit *The Dial,* a journal devoted to transcendentalist thought), activist Dorothea Dix (who became superintendent of army nurses during the Civil War), and others also contributed their talents. Bronson's Temple School was fertile ground for philosophers and social activists.

The new September term opened with double the students. Forty young voices now conversed under the high ceiling at the Temple School, and on Bronson's thirty-sixth birthday—and Louisa's third—in November 1835, the school hosted a party.

The students presented their teacher with a copy of John Milton's epic *Paradise Lost.* One girl recited an ode, and another a formal address. Bronson reflected aloud on his life so far, and afterward, decked in a crown of flowers, Louisa had the honor of standing on the teacher's big desk and handing out refreshments: plum cakes.

As the stragglers came up to make their claim, it dawned on Louisa that there wouldn't be enough to go around.

"The cakes fell short," Louisa recalled later, "and I saw that if I gave away the last one I should have none. As I was queen of the revel, I thought I ought to have it, and held it tightly."

"It is always better to give away than to keep the nice things," Abby urged softly, nudging her daughter to do the right thing, however wrong the right thing felt. "I know my Louy will not let the little friend go without."

"The little friend received that dear plummy cake," wrote Louisa later, "and I a kiss and my first lesson in the sweetness of self-denial—a lesson which my dear mother beautifully illustrated all her long and noble life."

In truth, it wasn't the first lesson for Louisa. It certainly wouldn't be the last.

Tuesday November 10

—

Phenomena and Observations.

I saw them less to-day than usual.
They were with their mother in the Nursery:
She informed the they were happy; interested
in each other, and in their recreations — differed
but little, and were generally obedient. Anna
has taken the work of self-culture into her
own hands already, is interested in the study
of her own ideas and feelings, desires, and is ambitious to deserve, the affection of her parents;
and has uniformly acknowledged her errors
voluntarily. To-day, she said to me, when
I came from School, "Father I have done
one naughty thing since you went away, but
I do not need punishing". She makes a
distinction between punishment, and its
purpose — improvement — amendment

⇛ 3 ⇚

WITHOUT
COMPASS
OR CHART

1835-1836

This reminds me . . . of my Louisa's definition of patience.
Her father was eating a piece of Gingerbread. She wanted
a piece of his (having finished her own). He told her she
could not have any more until afternoon, and that she
must wait patiently. Do you know what patience is?
said he. Yes, said L, it means wait for gingerbread.

—Abigail May Alcott, journal, September 1835

*T*he record-cold winter of 1835 kept Boston Harbor—and all other eastern harbors from New York to Nova Scotia—frozen solid much of the time. The eaves of the state capitol hung with icicles. There was no shortage of snow that winter, and hooting schoolboys had epic snowball fights on Boston Common. Sleigh bells rang, and frozen fingers, noses, and ears were common medical complaints, especially if you had the misfortune to be a stagecoach driver on the eastern route.

Bronson's Temple School boasted just one stove—not up to the challenge of warming the sixty-foot schoolroom or its pupils. But the teacher vowed to "kindle a fire for the mind" and seems to have succeeded, as his teaching methods that season made him one of the most celebrated men in Boston.

Meanwhile, at home, Abby was overworked, isolated, and exhausted. With the new baby and two warring imps, ages four and three, vying for her attention night and day, she was doling out spankings and on the verge of emotional collapse.

Bronson knew that Anna and Louisa were out of control. He worried that Abby had lost her early enthusiasm for motherhood—that she was failing to "seize the happiest moment, or the best means," while he was neglecting his duties as a father. The results, he wrote, were "disastrous."

"Without me," he concluded, "they soon lose their tranquility: they irritate each other—Anna unconsciously, Louisa intentionally."

Though younger than Anna, Louisa was tougher and ruled the nursery with brute force.

Anna needed protection from Louisa, "who from the mere love of action often assaults her sister and looks on to see what will be the result of her temerity." Bronson wrote that Anna often bore "the mark of her sister's hand" on her cheek, and flew to her mother "for protection."

With the school up and running, Bronson resolved to ease Abby's domestic burden and spend more time with the girls.

Welcoming Anna and Louisa into his study, he would pause in his work to trace their hands or feet into his notebooks or read them fables. At night he ran leisurely baths, had them narrate their days' adventures, and gave them unhurried time to play before tucking them in.

At home, as at school, Bronson saw play as a means of teaching. He taught Louisa to identify letters as patterns that her body could shape. He would lie on his back and lift his legs to make a *V*, and she would copy him as he spoke the letter and she shouted it. He would then lean a leg to meet her foot, and say,

"*W.*" He had his girls strut like geese around the room, hissing "Sssss" to make the sound of the letter *S.*

Even as a small child, Louisa wore her future calling as a writer like a cape. She flipped through her parents' books before she could decipher them, and sat in her little chair poring over pictures for a half hour at a time, pretending to read. She made buildings and bridges with the big dictionaries and volumes of history in the family library. "In moods of quiet," Bronson wrote, "she is most interesting. . . . Her thoughts come rushing after each other . . . so fast and so evanescent . . . all clear and vivid to her."

He described Louisa's energy in acting out the dramas from the tales he read aloud to her. A quick study with spoken language, she had a rich vocabulary, appreciating "all relations of expression," he wrote, "using every part of speech."

How could he tame and direct all this into a noble purpose?

In place of stern threats or spankings, Bronson tried gentle reason. He asked the girls, as he did his students at the Temple School, to weigh their punishments in light of the crime.

If Louisa threw her food, he sent her to bed without supper, explaining why. When she pinched Anna and pulled her hair, Bronson summoned her over: "Anna says that you took hold of her hair so, and pulled her hair . . . and that you pinched her cheek so . . ." By mimicking her behaviors, he let her connect the dots herself and hopefully helped her conclude that hurting her sister had been naughty. He asked the girls to study their motives: Did they want to be good merely to avoid punishment, or because it was the right thing to do?

Conversation, reason, and patient affection worked wonders with Anna—who couldn't bear criticism or discipline and who longed, above all, for approval. "Could I have her under my influence continually," Bronson wrote, "and provide suitable aid for her mother in the performance of domestic duty, I could shape her into the image of my desires. Not so Louisa."

"One builds; the other demolishes," he lamented.

Louisa's personality, so unlike his own, continued to baffle Bronson. "Louisa and Anna have separate claims upon my affections, but I have rather more sympathy with Anna's nature," he observed. "Louisa has a noble heart. The right love and look penetrate her, but her *force* makes me retreat sometimes from an encounter." She was thorny and defiant no matter what he tried, and her "ferocity" and "deep-seated obstinacy of temper" kept the household in an uproar.

Louisa's world—and her opportunity for mischief—opened up in the spring when Bronson, secure in the school's success, moved the family to a small but well-appointed house on Cottage Place on the south side of Boston Common. Louisa's ongoing restlessness and violence, Bronson wrote, was "at times alarming," but of equal concern was her wanderlust.

While her father was at work and Abby attended to her large household (the Alcotts took in a family of boys to board and tutor during this time frame as well), Louisa, not yet four years old, learned to slip out and explore the neighborhood. Reflecting later, Louisa recalled having "impromptu picnics . . . on the dear old Common, with strange boys, pretty babies, and friendly dogs, who always seemed to feel that this reckless young person needed looking after." Her toddler self shared "many a social lunch" with "hospitable Irish beggar children, as we ate our crusts, cold potatoes, and salt fish on voyages of discovery among the ash heaps of the waste land that then lay where the Albany station now stands."

Some adventures were more harrowing than others, like the time Louisa got a pair of new green shoes and set out to show them off. First she showed the cat. Unsatisfied, Louisa slipped out and showed the flowers in the yard. She displayed her shoes for pigeons, but that didn't satisfy her either. Louisa opened the gate and strolled down to the wharf, and modeled her footwear for sailors.

Having lost track of time, and feeling disoriented, she plunked down on a doorstep to rest, hopelessly lost.

"The town-crier found me fast asleep at nine o'clock at night" on a Bedford Street doorstep, she wrote, "with my head pillowed on the curly breast of a big Newfoundland."

Since the move to Boston, Louisa had set sail on an

"impetuous stream of instinct," her father understood. She wanted what she wanted—now—and to get it, she steered her ship "proudly, adventurously, yet without compass or chart." For her own sake, he thought, she must be tamed.

But no matter what measures Bronson took to form her character, Louisa remained aggressively impatient, pursuing her purpose by any means. He even imagined that he saw in her instinctive nature "signs of impending evil."

Louisa *was* passionate in her attachments, and loyal, he admitted, but when Bronson wasn't blaming her willfulness on a carnivorous diet (he was a vegetarian before there was a word for it), he hinted that Louisa's temperament might just be her mother's fault.

Abby, with a temper of her own, was the closest model at hand. A loving and capable mother, fiercely devoted to her children, she remained a firm supporter of her husband's theories of child development. But she couldn't always meet his high standards. Reluctant to discipline the girls, or too tired to carry out positive discipline, Abby often left punishment to Bronson, who took credit when things went well but blamed bad behavior on an "inadequacy of maternal culture."

To keep peace, he sometimes brought Anna to school with him, which restored domestic harmony but also made it clear that Anna was his child and Louisa her mother's.

Once drawn, this line would not be undrawn.

Bronson's at times stubborn sense of authority was not lost on Elizabeth Peabody, who still boarded with the Alcotts, ate at their table, and played with baby Lizzie.

At first, she had found the situation ideal and the family to be good company, but Peabody had learned that Bronson couldn't tolerate dissent, and that his wife was quick to the defensive and quicker to anger, too proud to see or accept blame on behalf of herself or her family.

The couple began to find Peabody, in turn, "offensively assertive," and a rift soon developed.

Over the course of the 1835–1836 school year, Peabody came to doubt Bronson's approach to teaching, too—especially his habit of inviting students to defy him and then shaming them in public.

His methods were gentle, but he could be autocratic and strict, she observed, taking a lofty tone and dismissing views different from his own. Most disturbing to his colleague, he didn't seem to know how to rein it in—or care—when public opinion turned against him.

And very soon, it would.

≫4≪

POOR
AS
RATS

1836–1840

I have often been taught by what very
small children have said; and astonished
at their answers. . . . Has truth any age?
All wisdom is not in grown-up people.

—*Amos Bronson Alcott*, How Like an Angel Came I Down

*A*fter the success of Elizabeth Peabody's *Record of a School,* Bronson hoped to collaborate on another volume of his conversations with students.

Peabody supported the idea, but his intended focus, a dialogue about the life of Christ, worried her.

In *Record of a School,* Bronson had let the schoolchildren speak for themselves. The results had been spontaneous and genuine. This time around, though he was still using the children's words, he seemed more interested in shaping the discussion to support his intellectual agenda. Peabody felt that by revising her notes—an assistant's careful transcript of actual classroom conversation—Bronson was compromising the integrity of the project.

A passage about Christ's miraculous birth that strayed to the topic of biological birth also greatly concerned Peabody. The discussion had prompted Josiah Quincy (the six year old son of Harvard's acting president) to reflect on the "naughtiness" of making babies. The dialogue that followed might be viewed as sex education for young children, Peabody cautioned, a scandalous idea in Victorian Boston. Bronson was less concerned.

But it was a personal blow that finally sent Elizabeth Peabody packing. "Mrs. Alcott came into my room & looked over my letters from you & found your last letter to me & carried it to Mr. Alcott," she wrote to her sister Mary "—and *they have read them.*"

The Alcott daughters were used to such scrutiny: their childhood diaries were never quite private. But for Peabody, the sting of this invasion was too much to bear. She moved out, resigning her position at the Temple School. Her younger sister, Sophia, also an educator (who would marry the famous novelist Nathaniel Hawthorne in 1842), took Elizabeth's place both in the Alcott home and at school, transcribing Bronson's conversations with no objections.

When the first volume of *Conversations with Children on the Gospels* was published in 1836, it seemed that all of Boston was outraged.

Reviewers called the book "absurd," "indecent," and "obscene." They accused Bronson of being "radically false and mischievous" and even "insane" or "half-witted."

Alarmed parents began pulling students out of the school one by one, and by the spring of 1837, the school was down from forty scholars to ten.

Bronson's high-minded idealism had backfired on him. The last thing he'd intended was to corrupt his students with "blasphemy" or trigger a scandal. Only a year before, his innovative teaching style—which had not changed—had made him one of the city's most admired men.

It had taken him more than a decade to build his reputation as a visionary educator. With just a few pages of type, he had demolished it.

Fellow transcendentalists rallied to his defense—even Elizabeth Peabody, who rose above their personal differences to champion her former colleague. Bronson's crime, she argued, had been to challenge a status quo that imposed "the adult mind upon the young mind."

In a letter, Ralph Waldo Emerson told his friend Bronson, "I hate to have all the little dogs barking at you." But the damage was done. The gentle schoolmaster was too radical, even for intellectual Boston.

Bronson took his downfall calmly, even when people hissed at or stoned him as he passed. He could no longer cross Boston Common without being whispered about and jeered at. He felt isolated and alone and saw "not a single individual who apprehends my great purpose." His abrupt turn of fortune was breathtaking and the stain of dishonor hard to bear, though Bronson found dignity in confronting slander with "unbroken silence."

Abby marveled at his composure. "You have seen how roughly they have handled my husband," she wrote to her brother Sam. "He has been a quiet sufferer. . . . I rail, and he reasons and consoles me as if I was the injured one."

Bronson moved what was left of the school from the airy top floor of the Masonic Temple to a windowless basement room in the same building. He put the classroom's elegant furniture, globes, and busts of Socrates and friends on the auction block, along with some three hundred books from the school library. (Bronson had lovingly built the collection from scratch, often with borrowed money.) Many of the books were rare and beautiful leather-bound editions of classics; dearest of all, and hardest to let go, was his five-volume set of the dialogues of Plato.

The US economy was in a slump at the time, so not everything on the auction block sold, and nothing sold for what it was worth.

Despite the proceeds, Bronson came out of his Temple School experiment many thousands of dollars in debt.

When the sheriff arrived to collect the furnishings that had sold at auction, Louisa was with Bronson. Sensing his grief, she verbally attacked the culprit. "Go away, bad man!" she shouted, all bluster and fearsome loyalty. "You are making my father unhappy."

Two months later, in June 1838, the Temple School closed its doors once and for all.

That fall, when Louisa was six years old, she moved into her twelfth new home. The Alcotts left their genteel house near the

Common to share quarters with another family in a cramped South End apartment a few blocks away on Beach Street.

Bronson continued to teach the young, including his daughters, in a home school, and Louisa found a fast friend in housemate and fellow student Frank Russell, "to whom I clung," she wrote later, "with a devotion . . . he did not appreciate." The playmates "snuggled in sofa corners and planned tricks and ate stolen goodies."

Wandering Louisa was already familiar with Boston's streets and wharves. A bold urban girl to the core, she knew the city's sounds and smells and where to find adventure. But she and Frank found plenty right in their backyard, haunting a piano factory behind their apartment building on Beach Street. They'd climb into the carts used to transport heavy loads from room to room and, in her words, "go thundering" down the ramps, "regardless of the crash that usually awaited us at the bottom."

Frank admired Louisa's pluck and pride and would play-slap at her hands with books, chopsticks, shoes—anything he could think of. "She's a brave little thing," he would pronounce, "and you can't make her cry."

All the same, he and the other boys wouldn't let her play football on the Common with them. Girls were banned from team sports—even active, competitive girls like Louisa, who always imagined herself "a deer or a horse in some former state, because it was such a joy to run." No girl who "refused to climb trees, leap fences, and be a tomboy" could be her friend, she wrote, and no boy "till I had beaten him in a race."

Louisa's loyalty was fierce, but not as fierce as her pride. Frank won and lost Louisa's friendship in equally spectacular fashion. "I did something very naughty," she wrote, "and when called up for judgment fled to the dining room, locked the door, and from my stronghold defied the whole world."

Frank, whether under adult pressure or for the sake of justice, "climbed in at the window," she wrote, "unlocked the door, and delivered me up to the foe."

"That nearly broke my heart," she lamented, "for I believed *he* would stand by me as staunchly as I always stood by him." Louisa scorned him from then on. "Peanuts and candy, gingersnaps," even football, couldn't "reunite the broken friendship."

Left out of the boys' games, Louisa "revenged" herself by rolling her toy hoop at breakneck speed through Boston's parks, a feat no boy could match—and it nearly got her killed. One day as she was showing off in the Public Garden, Louisa and her speeding hoop careened right into the frog pond. She felt the murky water close over and choke her, but then a courageous African American boy plucked her from the depths.

Later, Louisa quipped that his heroism made her an abolitionist at a tender age.

The controversy over slavery riveted 1830s Boston, and her parents and their circle were part of the movement to abolish the institution. Abby and her brother Sam were among the earliest Northern abolitionists.

Bronson had been a traveling salesman in his youth, witnessing the injustice of Southern slavery firsthand, and belonged to the Anti-Slavery Society founded by his brother-in-law and others. With his school in shambles but his ideals intact, Bronson would again prove shockingly ahead of his time—and ahead of popular opinion—by admitting a student named Susan Robinson into their modest home school. She was African American.

The other parents sent a representative to confront Bronson. They wanted "the dismissal of the Robinson Child," he reported in his journal. "I decline."

Overnight, his student body evaporated, leaving only his daughters, Frank Russell, and Susan Robinson.

Bronson would never be hired as a teacher again.

"We are poor as rats," Abby wrote to Sam in October 1839. The family was struggling to get by on handouts of clothing, food, and money.

Through this and other times of hardship and reduced social standing, Abby stayed loyal to the dreamer she had married for love. Nicknamed "the Hoper" by his mother, Bronson seemed unconcerned with the family's mounting poverty. He had always prized ideas more than worldly things, she understood, from the day he turned up—tall, gracious, and full of visions for inspiring children's minds and spirits—at her brother's door, which Abby had chanced to open. Samuel Joseph May at that time had been a leading supporter of educational reform, women's rights, and abolition—a promising contact for the young visionary who would become his brother-in-law.

When Bronson declared his intentions to marry Abby, Sam had reassured the future bride: "Don't distress yourself about his poverty. His mind and heart are so much occupied with other things that poverty and riches do not seem to concern him."

Now, Abby began taking in sewing to support the family.

For Louisa's seventh birthday that November, Abby plied her needle to make her middle daughter a new doll. The old one, the precious companion of Louisa's first seven years, had "been through a good deal. Her head had been cut off (and put on again); she had been washed, buried, burnt, torn, soiled and banged about till she was a mournful object."

Bronson's gift to Louisa was a letter in his elaborate handwriting. "You are seven years old today. . . . You have learned a great many things since you have lived in a body, you feel your conscience and have no real pleasure unless you obey it." Louisa was working hard to be "always GOOD," her father acknowledged. What he didn't say was that for Louisa it was very often a losing battle.

Bronson was fighting his own battle. Disgraced and penniless, he grew depressed. Ralph Waldo Emerson sent money to cover pressing expenses and invited Bronson to move to Concord, about twenty miles west of Boston. Emerson even offered to pay the fifty-two-dollar annual rent that his neighbor Edmund Hosmer was asking for use of half his cottage near Emerson's stately white house off the Lexington Road. Emerson imagined Bronson making his living by "his own spade" as a farmer-philosopher.

Emerson had a habit of subsidizing his famous intellectual friends—offering work and gifts of money, cosigning loans, and volunteering use of his land and property—all to keep the people he admired close and the ideas flowing. No friend benefited more from Emerson's generosity over the years than Bronson.

The beleaguered Alcotts agreed that the move to Concord would be a fresh start. And the truth was, they had no choice.

In early April, with Abby again pregnant, the family loaded their humble belongings onto the stagecoach at Earl's Tavern on Hanover Street, and set out for Concord.

≈5≈

THE
LITTLE
KINGDOM

1840

She wasn't a willfully naughty child . . .
but very thoughtless and very curious.
She wanted to see every thing, do every thing,
and go every where: she feared nothing.

—Louisa May Alcott, "Poppy's Pranks"

*L*ouisa woke in their new home on Main Street to a frigid April Fools' Day and a scene of fairy brilliance.

An early-spring ice storm had covered the world in a crust, and the view from the windows of the cozy cottage owned by Mr. Hosmer—the Alcotts called it Dove Cottage—had the girls "in rapture," Abby wrote.

Louisa would remember as idyllic the three years in that simple brown house, a palace compared to their cramped rooms in Boston, and Bronson led them into the new life in Concord with hope and optimism, though his departure from Boston smacked of exile. The sting of scandal and defeat hung on, and within the family, he made no effort to hide his wounded feelings.

"Father told us how people had treated him," nine-year-old Anna wrote in her journal, "and why we came to live at Concord, and how we must give up a good many things that we like. . . . I fear I shall complain sometimes." But the community and surroundings became a welcome refuge for the beleaguered Alcotts.

Concord at the time was the epitome of a quaint New England township: artfully clustered white clapboard houses ringed round by woods and fields, with the Sudbury and Assabet Rivers running together to form the Concord River. It was here that patriot Paul Revere made his midnight ride, signaling the arrival of the British and the start of the American Revolution; one of that war's famous battles was fought at the town's north bridge.

That early spring of 1840, when the family arrived, the last ice on the river and on nearby Walden Pond yawned and cracked loudly. Long-legged birds stalked through thawing marshes. Cardinals and finches brightened the air. An explorer traipsing the river's banks might surprise a beaver or upset a row of turtles sunning on the rocks.

The Hosmer children next door (three of the five aligned in age with the Alcott girls) proved fine expedition partners for Anna, Louisa, and Lizzie. Louisa was always the "leader in the fun," Lydia Hosmer wrote, running down the road rolling a toy hoop "higher than her head" and eager to shock people with her independent ways.

Louisa adopted Cyrus—a year younger than she—as her favorite Hosmer. "Cy was a comrade after my own heart," she wrote. "We kept the neighborhood in a ferment by our adventure and hair breadth escapes."

Cy didn't get into scrapes himself but had "a splendid talent for deluding others into them." He coaxed Louisa to jump off the highest beam in the barn. (She sprained both ankles.)

He got her to rub her eyes with red peppers (then gallantly escorted her home in her blindness). Persuading her that the piglets would die in agony if their tails were not snipped off, Cy had Louisa "hold those thirteen little squealers while the operation was performed." She wrote later, "Those thirteen innocent pink tails haunt me yet."

More than ever, Louisa "wanted to romp and shout." She wanted to "slide down the banisters, and riot about." These urges, at times, put her in real danger. Whether piercing her foot with a pitchfork when leaping into the hay or eating tobacco on a dare (Abby fetched the gut-sick little girl home in a wheelbarrow), Louisa kept herself and her friends entertained—and her family on edge.

Louisa and Anna brought the Hosmers into their first theatrics, fitting up the ramshackle barn behind the house in order to stage dramatized fairy tales or melodramas—Anna took the damsel-in-distress roles while Louisa played the witch or a villain twirling his mustache. "Our giant came tumbling off a loft," she wrote, "when Jack cut down the squash vine" to protect his magic bean.

Pregnant Abby relaxed into the comparative serenity of their new environment while Bronson went to work planting a vegetable garden.

Much of Concord viewed the eccentric Alcotts from a

distance, with wary curiosity, but their intellectual circle stopped in regularly at the cottage for enlightened discourse. Friends found Bronson enchanted by the poetry of his rustic new existence—self-reliant and close to the earth, immune to industrial and consumer concerns—the very essence of transcendentalism.

According to his journal, he and Abby did "all that farmers and farmers' wives find necessary." It was a free and dignified life, he believed, and his friend William Ellery Channing agreed. The idea of Bronson hiring himself out for day labor while still living the philosopher's life of the mind impressed Channing.

"'Orpheus at the plough,'" Channing wrote of his rustic friend, "is after my own heart."

Anna began studies at Concord Academy while Louisa and Lizzie had lessons from a Miss Mary Russell at the home of Ralph Waldo Emerson. It was here that Louisa met Bronson and Emerson's friend Henry David Thoreau, who often led packs of children on expeditions into the woods and meadows of Concord. The Alcott sisters and friends ran free outdoors, mostly unsupervised and with Louisa leading the charge, but a day out with Thoreau was special.

Rabbits and squirrels didn't seem to mind the twenty-three-year-old schoolteacher, she observed, "any more than if he was a tree." Thoreau knew when flowers would bloom and when bees wouldn't sting. He could "make the birds come to him" or whistle to a snake so it listened. While he set his charges gathering lichens and berries, he might point out a fox den or deer tracks or stoop to feed a chipmunk from his hand.

Scientific in his view of nature, Thoreau also had a poet's eye for language and could spin a yarn. Tanagers set the woods ablaze, he told the children. Fronds of goldenrod drooped like medieval banners on crusade. A cobweb, for Louisa's amusement, became a fairy's handkerchief.

One of Louisa's favorite pastimes was paddling Thoreau's little boat, *Musketaquid,* along the Sudbury and Assabet Rivers. As the party drifted through historic Concord, Thoreau might narrate how local farmers had defended themselves against redcoats during the American Revolution. Often he just sat alert in the stern, playing his flute.

With his "massive head, covered with waves of ruddy brown hair, and gray eyes that "pierce[d] through all disguises," Thoreau seemed to Louisa to say more with silence than others did with words.

Floating in "still water," he wrote in his journals of the time, "I too am a planet and have my orbit, in space, and am no longer a satellite of the earth." Joy, Thoreau maintained, "is the condition of life."

Like her mystic mentor, Louisa seemed to harmonize with

the landscape, Bronson observed. She hung from the branches of elm trees, scaled fences, and, whenever she got the chance, rambled far from the scholarly discipline that he insisted on at home. Bronson believed in the instructive power of nature and the imagination, like all good transcendentalists, but he also withheld enjoyment when the girls neglected their lessons.

Much later, Louisa would call Concord "one of the dullest little towns in Massachusetts," but with residents like Thoreau, Emerson, Margaret Fuller, and on-and-off resident Nathaniel Hawthorne, the town deserved its reputation at the time as the heart of literary America. Surrounded by great books and authors, both male and female—and encouraged to question, play, and dream—Louisa could allow her imagination to bloom.

When she turned eight, she began to keep a more formal journal, which included her early efforts at poetry. As ever, both parents read and commented on her writing, and Louisa and Abby often wrote little notes back and forth in her journal.

As wild and impetuous as ever, Louisa was (to herself as well as to others) still the "topsey-turvey" girl she had always been. But writing was a way of managing and reflecting on her moods and actions. In one telling poem, she tackled her biggest challenge—holding her emotions in check:

A little kingdom I possess,
Where thoughts and feelings dwell,

And very hard I find the task
Of governing it well . . .

Unable to accept that Louisa was so unlike him—that keeping her little kingdom in order could feel all but impossible at times—Bronson kept trying to curb her willful nature. She worked hard to tame her temper and find the peaceful paradise that her father swore lived inside her, but too often chaos ruled her, and her father's disappointment increased her anguish.

Like writing, reading helped Louisa cope with the disarray inside. She took comfort in characters, such as Charlotte Brontë's Jane Eyre, who were as passionate and willful as she was. Both parents saw educational value in stories, but Bronson used them to teach moral lessons, while Abby told sensational tales of witchcraft in Salem. (Abby's ancestor Samuel Sewall had been a judge during the witch trials.) Louisa's "Marmee" understood her daughter's nature, and nurtured what was best in Louisa while helping her manage the worst.

Perhaps because they *were* so alike (Abby could thunder and rage as well as or better than her middle child), Abby was especially protective of Louisa's feelings, doubling Bronson's frustrations. In one journal entry, he cast Abby and Louisa as "two devils" that he couldn't control or improve. "The mother fiend and her daughter" were "part of one another" and could not "be separated long at a time."

But separated they were when forty-year-old Abby, who had suffered many miscarriages over the years, approached childbirth once again that summer. She would need rest and calm, and her middle girl demanded too much care and attention, and acted out loudly when she didn't get it. "Two [children] make peace," Bronson explained to Anna, while three brought discord.

And so, just when Louisa had taken to country living, she found herself exiled to Boston to stay with Grandpa May.

In late June, not long after Louisa left, Bronson sent her an affectionate letter (with only a mild reminder to be good):

My Dear Louisa,

We all miss the noisy little girl who used to make house and garden, barn and field ring with her footsteps and even the hens and children seem to miss her. Be good, kind, gentle, while you are away, step lightly, and speak soft about the house; Grandpa loves quiet as well as your sober father, and other Grown people.

Elisabeth says often, "Oh, I wish I could see Louisa, when will she come home, mother? And another feels so too. Who is it?

Your Father.

But letters from home describing the births of new baby chicks and kittens in the hay—all the fun and frolic happening in Concord without her, on account of a baby she hadn't met yet—must not have been much consolation.

Forlorn Louisa "longed to see mamma" and pestered her distinguished guardian with questions such as "Grandpa, why don't you have any hair on the top of your head?"

She took to visiting a big empty room upstairs in his house at the corner of Washington and Oak Streets downtown. Her "great delight was to lean out of the window as far as she could, and look at the people in the street, with her head upside down. It was very dangerous, for a fall would have killed her; but the danger was the fun."

Grandpa did his best, and six weeks later, Louisa arrived home by stagecoach to find a baby with golden hair and blue eyes cradled in Marmee's arms.

Concord June 21st 1840.

Dear Mother,

I write from my little cottage in
Concord, (18 miles from Boston) into which we moved
on the first of April last, ~~and~~ to find much happiness
by this change from the city to the country. I
cultivate a garden and a field, in all about
an acre and three quarters, and find constant
occupation on this my frail farm: my vegetables look finely at this time. I shall raise
more than a supply for my family. Abba does
all her work and the children all go to school in
the village close by, and we are free to do all

≈6≈

"WHAT MAKES ME SO HAPPY?"

1840-1843

A philosopher is a man up in a balloon,
with his family and friends holding the ropes which
confine him to earth and trying to haul him down.

—*from* Louisa May Alcott: Her Life, Letters, and Journals

*T*he girl born on July 26, 1840, was called "Baby" for several weeks before she was given her mother's name.

"My baby is a sweet little creature," Abby wrote to her brother Sam, "and the children aid me a good deal in the care of her; Anna assumes a thousand little responsibilities concerning her and Elizabeth is full of tender care. Louisa serves me in the way of dishes and cleaning as better suiting her genius."

Abigail May (later just "May") would always be the baby of the family. With a hint of envy, Louisa eventually came to call the last-born Alcott the "lucky" one. May didn't spend her formative years as the subject of an experiment, for one thing. Her father had moved on to other intellectual pursuits by then and kept no journal of her development.

When young May joined the Alcott brood, Bronson was consumed with ideas about communal living and cooperative labor. Intrigued by Reverend George Ripley's experimental Brook Farm, a utopian community in nearby West Roxbury (for a time, the writers Nathaniel Hawthorne and Margaret Fuller were both residents), Bronson paid the colony a visit. He was dismayed that the colonists ate meat and wore leather. Like

Emerson, who had already politely declined an invitation to join Brook Farm, Bronson found the colony's party atmosphere of dancing, card playing, charades, dramatic readings, and costume balls a bit distracting, and not conducive to spiritual study. And besides, he couldn't afford the five-hundred-dollar share payment.

But utopian philosophy had taken hold of him.

Bronson's lofty ideals and moral imperatives had long depended on Abby's tireless labor and her gift for making do on nothing, but now more than ever his dignified front disguised the family's dire straits. In a letter to her brother Sam, Abby admitted that Bronson's ample garden might keep the family from starving come winter, but only just. "If it would pay our rent and give us shoes and bread we should not have to ask charity or receive advice."

Though her brother was generous and empathetic, Abby resented having to beg financial assistance from him. "I would sometimes be thought of as other than a beggar," she confessed to Sam. "I experience at times for whole days the most exquisite sense of weariness. I cannot get rest. I feel like a noble horse harnessed in a yoke, and made to drag and pull instead of trot and canter."

When her father, Colonel Joseph May, died at age eighty in February 1841, Abby learned that he had put her portion of his estate in trust to her brother and a male cousin, which prevented

Bronson from claiming the money toward his debt. Bronson's creditors would sue the estate and send the money into probate for three years. Abby could not claim her inheritance.

After the will was read, stung by what she perceived as a betrayal, she wrote, "My father did *not* love me."

Abby was whip-smart with a barbed wit but far too burdened at home to teach or write professionally, as other women in her circle did. As the family slipped out of genteel poverty and into the desperate kind, she took in work as a seamstress, vowing, "My girls shall have trades."

Emerson too was alarmed by the family's predicament. When stopping by the cottage for a visit, he would discreetly slip money between sofa cushions or under a candlestick. He even offered to have the Alcotts move into his home in Concord. Abby was grateful but knew that the arrangement wouldn't work. She was too proud and temperamental, she wrote to Sam, to labor "in another person's yoke." She would take in more sewing.

Louisa lived a life of paradoxes: she had two loving, attentive parents who could barely meet her basic needs. Rich in intellectual wealth—surrounded by prominent thinkers, teachers, and spiritual leaders—and hailing from old Boston wealth and influence on their mother's side, Louisa and her sisters nonetheless grappled daily with poverty.

At nine years old, Louisa's moods mirrored these polarities. Though full of fun and mischief and with "great firmness of purpose and resolution" one day, she could display "the greatest volatility and wretchedness of spirit" the next. Sometimes, Abby lamented, Louisa seemed to lose all hope, all heart, and sink into darkness, becoming "sad solemn and desponding."

Abby was having a hard time hoping—and coping—herself. She both defended Bronson's honor and integrity against outside attack and quietly railed: "Why [does he] so much take, take, [and] so little Give! Give!" To Sam she confessed, "My dear brother. . . . It is this dependence on others which is the worm gnawing at the vitals of my tranquility. . . . Fuel must be *paid* for. . . . What is to be done?"

By the spring of 1841, only five-year-old Lizzie was still enrolled in school. Anna and Louisa, and their labor, were needed at home. Like Abby, Louisa was a deft seamstress. She "plies her hands nimbly with her mother," Bronson wrote, "or flies like a bird over the garden." As summer turned to fall, Louisa flew around the grounds gathering apples for winter while her father cut firewood for neighbors.

One evening in November, Abby's cousin Hannah Robie came to visit. She wrote in her diary that she "did not dare go to Concord without carrying tea and coffee." With the dietary bans at Dove Cottage in mind, she would also smuggle in "a small piece of cooked meat, in case my wayward stomach should crave it."

When Robie arrived with a bag of old clothing that she'd

collected for the family (Abby cut up threadbare donations and reversed the fabric to stitch new dresses for the girls), she found the Alcotts eating a meal of bread and water. They seemed to be subsisting on bread, she learned—along with potatoes, apples, and squashes. What little the charitable family had, they divvied up with needy strangers. (The Alcotts had recently begun living on two meals instead of three; the children delivered their reserves to a struggling family living in a nearby "hovel.") Robie and Bronson argued over milk during her visit. He wanted to remove it from the family's diet entirely; the visitor felt that baby May needed it.

Robie brought news of the family's destitution back to Boston with her, but even concerned relatives were now refusing to lend the Alcotts money. Sam May, though sympathetic to his brother-in-law's ideals, couldn't fathom why Bronson wouldn't support his family without relying on friends and benefactors. Others had to labor, Sam reasoned in a letter to Abby, so why shouldn't Bronson?

Loyal but desperate, Abby admitted, "I believe he will starve and freeze before he will sacrifice principle to comfort. . . . I and my children are necessarily implicated." To her mounting despair, Bronson would only ask for donations—he would never charge wages—for his wood cutting and other day labor.

As Thanksgiving drew near, Abby found herself craving "pick-bones and cranberry sauce." But there would be no

Thanksgiving turkey that year. The whole family now followed the vegetarian principles of Sylvester Graham, inventor of the graham cracker, and gave thanks over a platter of apple pudding.

"My children are beginning to be objects of great solicitude to me," Abby wrote in her journal that December. "I feel sometimes as if great obstacles had been thrown in their way especially to arouse my own energies and bring out and confirm the great and good in them. They are fine girls . . . generous and fearless."

The Alcott financial bind was an open secret, and even Emerson was losing patience. He maintained that his friend's lofty ideals—and tendency to talk instead of act —were turning Bronson into a "tedious archangel."

But talk was Bronson's medium, and he was still commissioned to host the odd public conversation. Not quite a lecture and not quite an open discussion, nineteenth-century conversations were guided forums held at an athenaeum (a cultural assembly hall or library) or in the parlor of a leading citizen. Led by a scholar—usually a man, though Margaret Fuller's sessions were extremely popular—these conversations focused on a theme such as civil disobedience or free will. The discussions were often hosted as a series and paid for by subscription, and were a night on the town for intellectuals.

With his regal bearing, ethereal blue eyes, and hypnotic voice, Bronson was "serene and lofty" in his deportment, as Emerson put it. He could still command a room and had little trouble finding an audience. But here again, Bronson rarely charged for his services. As when he chopped wood for his neighbors, he accepted donations for his talks.

With the garden offering only the barest subsistence living, and pressure mounting for him to provide for his family, Bronson grew depressed again.

"He will not long survive this state of things," Abby confided to Sam in a letter. If Bronson's body didn't fail, she feared, his mind would. "He experiences at times the most dreadful nervous excitation."

Emerson's young son Waldo died of scarlet fever around this time, and in his grief, the generous Sage of Concord drew back from Bronson, finding it harder to sympathize with his friend's plight and eccentricities. "Here is a fine person," Emerson wrote, "with wonderful gifts but mad as the rest & by reason of his great genius, which he can use as a weapon too, harder to deal with."

Emerson volunteered to fund a trip for Bronson across the Atlantic so that his friend could visit Alcott House, a school in England committed to his educational ideals and named in his honor. Emerson hoped it would inspire Bronson to new professional pursuits but also seemed surprised when his friend accepted. He marveled that Bronson was "quite ready at any moment to abandon his present residence and employment, his country . . . his wife and children, to put any new dream into practice."

Abby too understood that "wife, children, and friends are less to him than the great ideas he is seeking to realize," and tried to hide her disappointment behind a brave front. With no immediate allies to lean on other than the daughter she most identified with, Abby folded a clipping she had found of a sick mother attended by a loyal daughter into one of her notes to Louisa. The note read:

A picture for you which I always admired very much, for in my imagination I have thought you might be just such an industrious good daughter and that I might be a sick but loving mother, looking to my daughter's labors for my daily bread. Take care of it for my sake and your own because you and I have always liked to be grouped together.

There is no record of young Louisa's response, but as her father prepared to sail across the Atlantic on what many saw as a fool's errand, she must have felt as unsettled as her mother.

Abby saw little rhyme or reason in her husband's choices but packed him off for the voyage with loaves of graham bread, pots of applesauce, and crackers. Bronson's younger brother, Junius, came to live with the family at Dove Cottage in his absence, but still Abby mused, "It is with a trembling hand I take the rudder to guide this little bark alone." She felt ready for what would be a heroic chapter in her own and her children's lives, a time even more fraught with "hardships, doubt, fears, adversities" than the sacrifices of the past, which had been made "under poverty and debt, misapprehension and disgrace."

But once Abby received word that her husband had arrived safely in England, she exhaled, admitting, "I am enjoying this separation from my husband. . . . I feel lonely; at times my solitude seems insupportable, but his letters fortify me."

"I have not left you," Bronson wrote, "you have been my companion and company all the way, and have grown more and more precious to me." Their love letters back and forth made him feel that he was courting Abby again, and he understood that he had needed perspective to appreciate his family in all their sweetness and light.

Letter writing in general overtook Dove Cottage. Abby set up a family post office to encourage the girls to write. It gave her joy to see them leaving notes for her and for each other, and in her journal she wrote of her children, "I live, move, and have my being in them."

For May's birthday celebration in July, the Alcotts decorated the barn and took a happy rowboat outing with Junius. Abby reflected later in her journal, "I seldom omit these occasions for showing my children the joy I feel in their birth and continu-ance with me on earth. I wish them to feel that we must live for each other."

Bronson wrote with plans for a grand experiment in communal living: he would found a new social model, a "consociate fam-ily," where every individual was received and loved in fellowship. It would be a community where money was unknown and no creature would profit by the suffering of others.

Bronson and three British newcomers—Henry Wright, Charles Lane, and Lane's ten-year-old son, William—arrived at Dove Cottage in mid-October to a house scrubbed and deco-rated by four ecstatic Alcott girls and their mother. They had crafted a little shrine, garlanding Bronson's mini portrait with wildflowers and branches. Abby welcomed the English visitors warmly. In her journal on October 21, she wrote, "Good news for cottagers! Happy days these!! Husband has returned accom-panied by the dear English-men; the good and true. Welcome to these shores, this home!"

As the family showed Wright and the Lanes around Concord, Louisa—earnest, and elated to have her family back together again—asked, "Mother, what makes me so happy?"

Bronson too was inspired, brimming with enthusiasm for

his vision of a self-sufficient utopia where colonists would live in harmony and equality in a modern Eden.

A fellow philosopher and reformer, Lane had the funds and the personality to manage the experiment in communal living and immediately assumed control of its destiny. The pattern was established in Dove Cottage even before the official colony was formed: Bronson saw to the ideals, Lane managed day-to-day household affairs, such as diet.

Like Bronson, Lane ate no meat, but he was more than a vegetarian. He was a devoted vegan with extreme dietary and lifestyle restrictions. Going forward, milk, butter, coffee, tea, liquor, salt, cane sugar, molasses, and spices were strictly forbidden. Maple sugar was the one sweetener permitted, and there would be only water to drink. The house took on an "atmosphere of restriction and gloom," Abby wrote, veering sharply from her welcoming stance of a month before. "Circumstances most cruelly drive me from the enjoyment of my domestic life. I am prone to indulge in occasional Hilarity. But I seem frowned down into stiff quiet and *peace-less* order. . . . Perhaps I feel it more after this 5 months of liberty."

Louisa shared her mother's feeling of "suffocation." While the weather held, she burned off her energy outdoors, but when the cold came and the cottage grew crowded and tense, she took to shouting, slamming doors, and sliding down the bannister (only to sprain both ankles . . . again). Louisa broke a tooth swinging a flat-iron on a string, picked fights with Anna, bad-gered Bronson with questions and arguments, and was in general critical, reckless, and rude.

On her tenth birthday in November—and his forty-third—Bronson's gift to Louisa was a letter: "I live, my dear daughter, to be good and do good to all, and especially to you and your mother and sisters. Will you not let me?" He urged her, as ever, to try to be meeker, gentler—to not let "anger, discontent, impatience, evil appetites, greedy wants, complainings, ill-speakings, idleness, heedlessness, rude behavior" rule her, leaving "the poor misguided soul to live in its own obstinate, perverse, proud discomfort."

Abby, in contrast, gave Louisa a pencil case, hoping her gift would inspire her daughter's muse and bring forth "pure poetic fire." Abby's note assured Louisa that she was seen. "DEAR DAUGHTER . . . I observed you are fond of writing, and wish to encourage the habit. Go on trying, dear, and each day it will be easier to be and do good."

But Abby herself was fed up with trying. On Christmas Eve 1842, "toil-worn and depressed" at age forty-two, she left Dove Cottage and her "arduous and involved duties," bringing Louisa with her to enjoy a traditional Boston Christmas with her relatives. "We may be [away] from home for some weeks," Abby notified Bronson.

They were gone for only a few days, but in that time, the

fugitives sang carols under holly boughs, gorged on "bounteous stores" of forbidden food, enjoyed lectures and concerts, and watched as the candles were lit on Amory Hall's massive Christmas tree.

Abby's formidable old Boston clan—the Mays, Willises, Windships, and Sewalls—threw a lavish holiday. For the starved would-be utopians, it would have been a feast for the belly and the senses (overwhelming too in its material splendor—watching indulged cousins empty teeming stockings onto the floor and exclaim over new skates or a sled).

Without Abby, domestic life at Dove Cottage ground to a halt. Bronson wrote, pleading for her return, and when she consented to come back on New Year's Day, "quickened by a new spirit of confidence and love," their relations improved, though her chores remained, and life marched on at the same joyless meter as before.

The Alcott parlor continued to brim with visitors eager for word of the new Eden, men who ate up the family's stores and left a constant mess for Abby, whose ideals were tempered by the need to keep her family fed and healthy. "Give me one day of practical philosophy," she lamented. "It is worth a century of speculation and discussion." She didn't believe, as Bronson did, that Providence would provide. Abby had seen for herself that it didn't—or not nearly often enough—but still passionately supported her husband anyway, however impractical his ideas. She loved and admired him, and stood by him, riding out their unstable home life.

But could she and the children adapt to the kind of community Bronson imagined? Abby was one of the few people in the world who believed in his dream, Bronson confessed. So how could she doubt him?

Emerson refused to fund or participate in his friend's project. One of Emerson's English acquaintances, who met Bronson during his stay in London, compared the philosopher to the hapless Don Quixote, who gallantly rode at windmills with his lance, thinking himself a knight. He called Bronson the sort of man "no one can even laugh at without loving."

Emerson did love Bronson but confided to others, "I would as soon exert myself to collect money for a madman." Emerson complained that the would-be colonists' "whole doctrine is spiritual, but they always end with saying, Give us much land & money."

In the end, Emerson told Bronson, "You ask too much."

Emerson's unwillingness stunned Bronson, who had learned to take his friend's support for granted.

It was left to Charles Lane to invest his life's savings, about two thousand dollars, and free Bronson from his Concord debts so that the group could leave town. Lane's fellow Englishman Henry Wright, disillusioned with Bronson and Lane's philosophy (Wright liked food, for one thing), defected to a community near Boston, abandoning the project.

Even Abby, who was reluctant to move again and increasingly suspicious of Lane, let herself hope when the Englishman announced that he had found a suitable home for their utopia: a tract of land in Harvard, Massachusetts, about sixteen miles west of Concord, with nineteen acres of field, orchards, and woodlands.

It was already late spring, and it would have been prudent to delay the move until the following year, allowing ample time to make repairs to the property and plant crops. But if the Alcotts stayed in Concord for another ten months, bills and debts would mount again. Lane had no business contacts to help him find work. And besides, the idealists had vowed to swear off the sins of buying and selling.

They named their community Fruitlands, and if it succeeded, it would prove that people could live in harmony with nature—and each other—by forming kinder, simpler bonds. If it failed, it would be mean disillusionment for Bronson and his followers.

Abby steeled herself, writing, "I hope the experiment will not bereave me of my mind," and she reflected on their three "eventful" years in Concord, feeling both nostalgia for the past and wary curiosity about the future.

In a now established ritual, the family packed up their humble belongings to set out for the unknown.

THE
PATHETIC
FAMILY

1843-1844

And here his wife, unconverted but faithful to the end, hoped,
after many wanderings over the face of the earth,
to find rest for herself and a home for her children.

—Louisa May Alcott, "Transcendental Wild Oats"

*O*n June 1, 1843, seven travelers—four of them children—set out on a sixteen-mile journey that took up most of a long summer day.

Abby held baby May while Lizzie, two years old, nestled near her father, who held the horses' reins. Anna, twelve, and Louisa, ten, rode on a cart heaped with motley possessions and provisions. The woeful bust of Socrates—survivor of the Temple School auction—bumped along between them.

From time to time, Anna climbed down and walked beside the wagon awhile, though she and Louisa mostly rode on the cart, whispering excitedly or humming absent lullabies to their dolls.

Charles Lane walked the entire way from Concord, either because there was no room for him on the wagon or because he was practicing the self-denial he now tirelessly preached to his consociate family. His son, William, was already at Fruitlands with one or two early recruits, preparing for the new arrivals.

After leaving the main road to navigate a steep cart road, the party reached the remote property in time to catch a glimpse of Fruitlands bathed in buttery late-afternoon light.

Nestled in a deep green gorge that Bronson christened "the

bowl of Heaven," the bright-red two-story house hunkered with its ramshackle outbuildings on the rocky soil of the hillside. Abby compared it in size to a pigsty.

After trooping inside, the pilgrims gratefully consumed roasted potatoes, brown bread, and water that William Lane and the new recruits had prepared for them—served up "in two plates, a tin pan, and one mug," according to Louisa. Then, too weary to set up house, they spread blankets on the kitchen floor, camp style, and slept.

In the days to come, as the men took to the fields, Abby broke from cleaning, whitewashing, nail driving, and curtain hanging to stroll with her daughters along the ridge between the farmhouse and the woods. While she gathered wood chips and named the features of "our little territory . . . Hill, grove, forest . . . woodland, vale, meadow, and pasture"—Louisa and her sisters raced around picking wildflowers for bouquets.

Surveying a landscape lush in summer, Abby felt the old familiar surge of hope. The farmhouse and outbuildings begged for improvements, but a clamber up a steep five-hundred-foot ridge offered a grand view of the Nashua Valley and the hazy blue slopes of Mount Monadnock in the far distance. Meadows waved with black-eyed Susans and Queen Anne's lace. The wood line rang with the chatter of chipmunks. Bees and dragonflies hummed past. It was "all beautiful," transporting them from their "littleness," Abby wrote. "The soul expands in such a region."

If only the Alcotts could collect about them "the true men and women," she wrote, "putting away the evil customs of society and leading quiet exemplary lives," the experiment at Fruitlands might succeed.

But she also braced herself for the possibility that it might *not* succeed: "It will be some consolation that we have ventured what no others have dared."

The broad goals of the experiment, according to Bronson and Lane, were "simplicity in diet, plain garments, pure bathing, unsullied dwellings, open conduct, gentle behavior, kindly sympathies, serene minds." Bronson had worked hard to sell this inoffensive platform to relatives and friends, but few were willing to sign on to enter a utopia strictly defined by Bronson Alcott and Charles Lane.

Many, like Abby's cousin Hannah Robie, were familiar with the dietary restrictions instituted back at Dove Cottage, which had been a deterrent for Henry Wright, one of the original "English mystics" to arrive with Bronson from London. An animal diet polluted not only the body, Bronson preached, but the mind. "Vegetable diet and sweet repose," Louisa recorded dutifully in her journal, but "animal food and nightmare."

For Abby, the long list of forbidden ingredients made cooking worse than a chore. The group had left Concord with scant provisions: potatoes, dried fruit, peas, beans, and barley. With no flavoring or variety beyond foraged nuts and berries, their diet was a monotony of unleavened bread, porridge, water, and fruit or vegetables. Abby had her work cut out for her, though Bronson did try to shape the simple loaves of bread he made into animals to amuse the children.

At Fruitlands, the exploitation of any living creature was ungodly. No animal should be robbed of life and flesh: milk belonged to cows (and to toddler May—her mother insisted), eggs to chickens, wool to sheep, and silk to worms.

Cotton, a product of slave labor in the South, was banned; clothing must be made of linen, a natural fiber created from flax. Male colonists wore tunics and pants of Bronson's design, and bathed in the river. For Abby and the girls, he used sheets and clothesline to rig up an outdoor shower. Standing on a ladder, he poured icy water through a sieve onto bowed heads while the girls stamped and howled. "I rose at five and had my bath," Louisa enthused in her diary. "I love cold water!" The girls wore linen tunics and bloomers.

It was a simple life with simple rules, and at any one time, there might be sixteen crowded into narrow beds at the red farmhouse on the hill.

The Alcott girls slept under a low roof in the stuffy attic, in a crawl space around the main chimney. Tall Louisa had to duck to enter or cross the space, which was suffocatingly hot in summer and frigid in winter. The only light in the long room trickled in through small windows at either end.

Bronson and Lane had persuaded a handful of male recruits seeking fellowship and spiritual growth to try their luck at Fruitlands. (The sole woman colonist besides Abby—a Miss Anne Page from Providence, Rhode Island—wouldn't arrive until August.)

Young Samuel Larned took self-denial to the extreme; he had once survived for a year eating nothing but crackers. Isaac Hecker, another young recruit hungry for self-denial, had already done a stint at Brook Farm, the utopian community in West Roxbury. Charles Lane recorded that Hecker hadn't been impressed with the competing utopia and its "schoolboy, dilettante spiritualism."

Abraham Everett was a hermit, bitter about society and commerce, in part because relatives had once tried to commit him to an insane asylum and steal his inheritance.

Samuel Bower, an eccentric Englishman, believed heartily—

with Lane and Bronson—in the restorative properties of un-cooked food; he was also a nudist, or champion of naturism. Clothing, he maintained, was a barrier to spiritual growth. Advised to cover himself in a sheet near Abby and the children, Bower would slip out at sunset to make a feast for mosquitoes, relishing long strolls in the buff.

Joseph Palmer, an elderly farmer, wasn't a formal member but periodically visited the colony to lend his support. He wore a long, billowing beard at a time when it was not socially acceptable to do so. When a mob had jumped him and attempted to hold him down and forcibly shave it off, he had stabbed one of his attackers, and had then served time in jail. His experience with intolerance made him sympathetic to the Fruitlands experiment and to people who suffered for their principles.

But if these motley dreamers meant to form a self-sustaining fellowship, they were on a timeline.

Because of the promise of an orchard; a nearby forest of oaks and chestnuts; plentiful edible roots, berries, and nuts; and a stream and spring on the property, the experiment's leaders had predicted prosperity. In reality, there was no orchard; the isolated property had a few twisted old apple, cherry, and peach trees, but not nearly enough of them to justify the hopeful name "Fruitlands." More important, it was perilously late in the planting season. In Massachusetts, spring wheat is in the ground by the end of April. Potatoes should be in by the end of May. It was already June.

After the first few backbreaking days, Bronson and the other middle-aged farmhands in their loose linen tunics agreed that cattle, exploited or otherwise, would be a welcome addition to the team. Joseph Palmer came to the rescue with an ox (and a cow, for good measure).

Quickly, but not quickly enough, the men planted carrots, potatoes, beans, and turnips, and sowed fields of sweet corn, wheat, barley, and rye. At one point, a trio of colonists, acting independently, seeded a single field with three different grains. When they discovered their error, they laughed and proposed to "see what would come of it."

When practical Emerson came to visit in the summer, he scribbled a grim prophecy in his diary: "They look well in July. We shall see them in December."

Bronson the educator might have liked to play more of a role in teaching the children, but because he was the son of a New Hampshire farmer, with a background in agriculture, his services were sorely needed in the fields and gardens. So dour Charles Lane—whom Abby thought lazy—dominated lessons.

The library where the consociate family gathered for

instruction and other activities was the best room in the run-down house, decorated with paintings and photographs (and the bust of Socrates) that had survived the Alcotts' many moves and the Temple School auction. The room's shelves were lined with nearly a thousand books that Charles Lane had brought over with him from England. Many of the Englishman's lessons were on the theme of self-denial—*not* Louisa's favorite. "I like the farm," she wrote, "but not the school part or Mr. Lane."

Luckily for active Louisa, Bronson and Lane were transcendentalists; they believed in the teaching benefits of outdoor recreation and in the natural world as teacher. After morning chores and schoolwork, Louisa, Anna, Lizzie, and William Lane fanned out, weather permitting, to pick berries, collect firewood, or just play. They ran with arms wide, up and down the steep hill, laughing and shrieking. They romped and shouted in the echoing barn or in the woods, wrote poems for one another, and made up games.

Indoor play was more scarce, but alongside moral instruction, the family enjoyed card games in the evening or music and dancing. (Charles Lane played the fiddle—one joy he brought to the mix.)

Fruitlands was meant to be a community of equals, but for Abby, it was anything but. Often the sole adult female colonist at a time in history when women were charged with all domestic chores—"the yoke on woman," she lamented in her journal—

she was overworked and undervalued. Lane treated her like a servant, excluding her from key conversations about the colony's mission and goals. Her toil was endless and her role thankless.

When female recruit Anne Page arrived in August, Abby welcomed the extra pair of hands. In Louisa's account, Miss Page innocently asked her mother if the farm kept any beasts of burden. Abby quipped, "Only one woman!"

Wise to her mother's struggles—and to the fact that her father was in thrall to Lane, a humorless tyrant—Louisa cast the Alcotts as "the Pathetic Family" in her writing. The pencil case Abby had given Louisa for her tenth birthday was put to good use the year she was eleven.

It was at Fruitlands that Louisa first began keeping a serious journal. In it, she recorded her thoughts and dreams, the books she read, her lessons. She narrated her day's adventures—running in the wind and playing horse, dressing up as fairies with Anna and Lizzie in the woods, collecting red leaves. Louisa took stock of her growth: "I get to sleep saying poetry—I know a great deal." She reflected on the natural world: "As I went to bed the moon came up very brightly and looked at me. . . . That night, the rain made a pretty noise on the roof." And she recorded her fears and longings: "I read a story about 'Contentment.' I wish I was rich, I was good, and we were all a happy family this day."

But as both Louisa and Anna knew, their diaries were not

private. Their parents often read them and commented in the margins, and with Bronson determined at all times to morally instruct the family, thoughts that the girls wanted to keep for themselves were best left in the silence between the lines.

Anna's diaries were upbeat and calculated to please, while Louisa more often let her fluctuating moods seep through: "I was cross to-day, and I cried when I went to bed. I made good resolutions, and I felt better in my heart. If I only kept all [resolutions] I make, I should be the best girl in the world. But I don't, so I am very bad."

Possibly to escape the burden of truth and to ease her feverish imagination—and her boredom—Louisa began cooking up wild fantasies and dramatic tales for her sisters to act out. But more often, hemmed in by tension and discontent at Fruitlands, Louisa turned her gaze inward and wrote poetry.

Louisa had pasted the picture of the "sick but loving mother" and "industrious good daughter" into her journal months earlier, and for Marmee's birthday in October, Louisa composed a poem in her notebook alongside the clipping Abby had given her:

To Mother

I hope that soon,
dear mother,
You and I may be

In the quiet room my fancy
Has so often made for thee, —
The pleasant, sunny
chamber,
The cushioned easy-chair,
The book laid for your
reading,
The vase of flowers fair;
The desk beside the window
Where the sun shines warm
and bright:
And there in ease and quiet
The promised book you
write;
While I sit close beside you,
Content at last to see
That you can rest,
dear mother,
And I can cherish thee.

Louisa poured her empathy into a poem that imagined her mother living in peace and ease, with leisure to write a book while her "industrious good daughter" kept watch by her side.

All through those cold, hungry weeks of emotional stress, Louisa dreamed of relief, an end to poverty and despair—for herself and her family but especially for her mother, "the best woman in the world."

Louisa also reported peering into the dark of the fireplace one day to a find a cautious fugitive staring back at her. Like other Alcott residences, Fruitlands was a safe house, a stop on the Underground Railroad. Little is known or has been recorded about these activities, but Louisa noted that enslaved people on the run "were sheltered under our roof," and Abby's minister brother, Sam, was an activist and organizer who helped "over a thousand fugitives . . . reach Canada." Both Abby and Bronson supported Sam's abolition work.

There can't have been many resources to share with the concealed traveler. On August 28, Louisa wrote simply, "We had a dinner of bread and water."

It was a long, bleak fall, with the experiment fading fast. Isaac Hecker, the alumnus of Brook Farm, had already abandoned the experiment after only two weeks. Now other residents, enthusiastic in the leafy months of plenty, fled as winter threatened. There was never enough food for those who remained, and before long, rebel consociates were sneaking into the barn to milk the cow.

In the end, the only Fruitlands crop that succeeded was barley, and the colony nearly lost it.

Bronson and Lane were out on a mission to hunt up new recruits, and most of the other colonists apparently off-site, when a storm threatened. The season's barley crop was already cut in the fields, and if not harvested, the grain would be wrecked by rain. With no other farmhands to hustle the crop into the granary, Abby and the girls and young William Lane hurried outdoors with aprons, bedsheets, and baskets.

What they rescued would feed the colony for weeks, but with winter looming, Abby began to fear that her children might starve.

Things would indeed get worse, for all the Alcotts, before they got better.

While out drumming up replacement recruits, Bronson and Lane investigated a nearby Shaker community and found themselves drawn at once to the purity of the Shaker doctrine. The Shakers were a religious sect opposed to the traditional family structure and to reproduction. Children were adopted, not born, into the community. Men and women lived in separate quarters, worshipped apart, and spoke to one another only in the presence of a chaperone. If a family with children joined the Shakers, the offspring were removed from their parents' care to be nurtured by the whole community. The biological family was allowed to meet just once a year, briefly, under the supervision of an elder.

Lane began to hint that the colony should now abandon Fruitlands and join the industrious Shakers.

Winter was closing in—it would turn out to be the worst in a century, dumping a grand total of one hundred inches of snow into their isolated bowl of heaven—and Abby was in no mood to embrace a new social theory or pack up and move again. More to the point, motherhood was her life's purpose, a passionate bond not to be trifled with.

For all her reservations, Abby was a loyal and dutiful wife doing her best to trust her husband's vision for their family. When Fruitlands had launched in June, neighbors from the Shaker village had visited—along with other curiosity seekers—and had shown "a most loving disposition towards us," Abby recorded at the time in her journal. She and Anne Page now made a return call, walking a cold mile to witness the model community firsthand.

"Visited the Shakers," Abby wrote afterward. "I saw but little of their domestic or internal arrangements, [but] there is servitude somewhere," she reflected, "I have no doubt. There is a fat, sleek, comfortable look about the men and among the women there is a stiff, awkward, reserve. . . . Wherever I turn I see the yoke on woman in some form or another."

Louisa still spent much of her time happily outdoors. She was aware of mounting tensions within the farmhouse, but even when her parents argued over the Shaker settlement, she kept her composure. "Though it was unpleasant without," she wrote in her journal, "I was happy within."

She and Anna were at odds much of that year, and Louisa had few female allies in the colony besides Abby. "No one will be as good to me as Mother," she lamented when Abby left with Lizzie for a visit to Boston.

"I had a music lesson with Miss P.," Louisa wrote of Anne Page. "I hate her. She is so fussy."

Later, Louisa would poke fun at the eccentric cast of characters at Fruitlands, characters such as the man who liked to lie on the floor and "groan lamentably" when sad; race, leap, and sing with joy; or crow like a rooster in the middle of the night when "a great thought burst upon him." This "irrepressible being . . . believed emotions of the soul should be freely expressed," Louisa wrote, "and illustrated his theory by antics that would have sent him to a lunatic asylum, if, as an unregenerate wag said, he had not already been in one."

As the novelty of the colonists' quirks and antics wore off, and winter crowded in, Louisa found less to laugh about.

She can't have minded much when Charles Lane publicly scolded Miss P. and banned her from utopia. Miss P.'s crime—or "sad lapse of virtue," as Louisa put it in her account—was nibbling on a fish tail while visiting a friend outside the compound.

Soon only the Alcotts and Lanes were left at Fruitlands.

Lane went right on preaching about the sins of marital and

family bonds. In his journal, he complained of Abby's "peculiar maternal love," which blinded her "to all else." He urged Bronson to search his soul.

Fed up with conversations that seemed to exclude her and her girls, Abby refused at one point to take meals—meals she had prepared—at the same table with her adversary. Desperate to hold on to her husband and the father of her children, she mounted her own passionate appeals against Lane and his influence.

Lane, meanwhile, urged Bronson, in private, to abandon his family. True transcendence and divine love could be achieved only by severing bonds of flesh and blood and living without personal ties, Lane argued, as the Shakers did. Lane believed that family intimacy was "the very mischief" and that Alcott's attachment to his wife and daughters stunted his spiritual growth. Lane didn't try to outright force Abby out—the community functioned on her toil, for one thing—but communal resources were evaporating, and something had to give.

Oppressed by his options, Bronson withdrew into hollow silence.

"Father and Mr. L. had a talk," Louisa announced in her journal on November 20, and "asked us if *we* saw any reasons for us to separate. Mother wanted to, she is so tired."

An even darker mood emerged as supplies and firewood dwindled. There was no comfort to be had in the chill, drafty old house. Louisa and young William got sick. With the three adults in turmoil that November, and Anna and Louisa at each other's throats, Abby relieved the tension by sending Anna to board with relatives.

Despairing for the fate of the family and weary of running what she called "a Hotel where man and beast are entertained without pay, and at great expense," Abby asked herself continually, "Oh when will rest come?"

To her brother Charles she wrote, "I am not dead yet, either to life or to love." But Abby was out of patience.

She began to contemplate mutiny, writing, "I mean to take my cubs and escape."

At another anguished family meeting, Bronson once again spoke of leaving the family to pursue his spiritual development. On the evening of December 10, Louisa recorded, "Mr. L was in Boston and we were glad. In the eve father and mother and Anna and I had a long talk. I was very unhappy and we all cried. Anna and I cried in bed, and I prayed God to keep us together."

At the New Year, Abby spelled out her intentions. Bronson *must* choose: go and follow Lane, join the Shakers and lose his loved ones, or banish Lane and wholeheartedly place his family above his divisive friend.

To see his high ideals pitted against his devotion to his children drove gentle Bronson to the brink.

With the family destitute and near starvation, he couldn't

get out of bed. But in high winter, he made his choice. He chose the Pathetic Family.

Lane packed his bags in January 1844 and brought his son to live with the Shakers.

Abby wrote to Sam: "Mr. Lane's efforts have been to disunite us," but Bronson's love for her and for the children was "too strong."

Abby's husband, though, lay down on his bed and turned from the door. Profoundly depressed, Bronson refused to eat or speak. Teetering between sanity and madness, he had, it seemed, made up his mind to die.

As Louisa later told it, in her fictionalized record, the family waited breathlessly. "Days and nights went by." But at long last he roused himself. "My faithful wife," he said, "my little girls,—they have not forsaken me, they are mine by ties that none can break. What right have I to leave them alone?"

At long last, Bronson took in a little nourishment that night. The next morning, he held out a "wasted hand" to Abby, and she heard a "feeble voice cry bravely, 'Hope!'"

An idea that "dwarfed and killed" a man, Bronson later concluded in his journal, was one to let go . . . and simply grow from.

The last Fruitlands entry in Louisa's diary rings with her own solitary hope and relief in moving forward, with her family intact:

I wrote in my Imagination Book, and enjoyed it very much. Life is pleasanter than it used to be and I don't care about dying anymore. Had a splendid run, got a box of cones to burn, sat and heard the pines sing a long time. . . . Had good times and woke to think and watch the moon. I had a pleasant time in my mind, for it was happy.

≫ 8 ≪

THE MODEL CHILDREN

1844-1848

We are dreadfull wild people here in Concord,
we do all the sinful things you can think of.

—Louisa May Alcott, in a letter to Sophia Gardner

*T*he Alcotts found shelter with the neighboring Lovejoys. Abby had arranged, with support from Sam, for use of three cheerful rooms and the farmhouse kitchen for fifty cents a week. A brief sled ride down the rough trail from Fruitlands brought the Alcotts to "quite comfortable . . . winter quarters," Abby reported in her journal. But it was still temporary.

Left with nothing to his name, Bronson needed time to recover his losses, both emotional and financial. He kept up the rigid Fruitlands diet, still wore his linen leggings and tunics, and feverishly scribbled down ideas and visions while the life of the family went on quietly around him. Abby, meanwhile, layered the girls in warm donated clothing and plumped them up with meat and dairy products. Bronson's mind was in distress all that winter—"the brain was haunted," he wrote—leaving him "debilitated" when spring came and "unfit for common concerns."

During the dark season at the Lovejoys, Louisa and her sisters were bewildered by their father's behavior. To them, he had always been a serene figure, a model of self-control and softly spoken reason. To see him withdraw from the family—pacing at night, suffering unearthly visions, and hunched over his anguished scribbling—must have been beyond puzzling, frightening even. Abby did her best to hide her own sorrow and fear from her daughters. She confessed in her journal that she saw no way to return joy to their lives. "I scarcely know where to begin."

People outside looking in variously saw her husband's ambition and suffering as saintly, deluded, or even mad. Emerson sympathized with his friend but kept his distance. Any community that retreated from the world, he concluded of Fruitlands, risked becoming "an asylum to those who have tried and failed, rather than a field to the strong."

Community would prove a balm when the Alcotts relocated that spring to Still River, the nearest village, and rented half a house called Brick Ends. For twenty-five dollars a year, they would have a kitchen, four other rooms, and a garden. "Our home is humble," Abby wrote on April 24, "but we have much comfort and few responsibilities."

Bronson went to work sowing neat garden beds, and Abby rejoiced that he was finally up and about—taking part in common concerns and the life of the family.

In Still River, Louisa, Anna, and Lizzie had the rare experience of attending a town school, and were thrilled to find friends their own age—attachments that soon rivaled family ties in importance. Among these friends were the three Gardner children: Polly, Sophia, and Walter. (Louisa "married" Walter in the woodshed that spring, trailing an apron on her head for a veil; it was, she wrote, a "brief and tragical experience" that ended with the bride slapping the groom.)

Alcott playmate Annie Clark remembered later, "As sure as the sun shone and the skies were blue just so sure was an afternoon gathering on the grass plot in front of Brick Ends." Together the friends jumped rope, played ball, and rolled hoops around the yard while Abby looked on "like the guardian angel of the merry company . . . smiling benignly" on their "pranks."

Annie also recalled that Louisa, the ringleader, at times ruled with an iron fist. If she "got mad, she *could* be severe." At twelve years old, in the wake of the emotional stresses of Fruitlands, Louisa expressed herself violently at times, even against inanimate objects. Stunned neighbors were treated one afternoon to the spectacle of a chair dangling from one of Brick End's windows. Louisa had bumped into it while cleaning and hurt herself; the chair had then been summarily tried, sentenced, and hung.

Her explosive charisma enchanted fourteen-year-old Frederick Llewellyn Willis, an orphan boarding with his grandmother in Still River that summer. Fred soon persuaded his elderly guardian to let him lodge with the Alcotts.

Fred, Anna, and Louisa spent much of that freewheeling summer of 1844 splashing in a swimming hole called Bare Hill Pond or exploring the woods. "We christened a favorite nook, a beautiful rocky glen carpeted with moss and ferns and opening on the water's edge 'Spiderland,'" Fred remembered. "I was King . . . Anna was the queen, and Louisa the Princess Royal." He remembered Louisa's delight in all wild things, even the eight-legged variety. When spiders of the realm expired, Louisa conducted elaborate burial rites and built little monuments.

Motherless Fred was devoted to Abby, who shared her worries and tears with the young man. "No matter how weary she might be with the washing and ironing, the baking and cleaning," he wrote, she kept it hidden from the girls. With them, she was "always ready to enter into fun and frolic, as if she never had a care."

Fred was impressed with Bronson too, who seemed to him "strangely out of place" in their pragmatic era. Mr. Alcott's spontaneous monologues were a joy. "I have seen him take an apple on his fork," Fred wrote, "and while preparing it for eating, give a fascinating little lecture as to its growth and development from germ to matured fruit."

Louisa was "full of life and spirit," Fred recalled, "impulsive and moody, and at times irritable and nervous," but when she was free and in motion, she seemed to him "like a gazelle," "the most beautiful girl runner" he ever knew. Louisa fearlessly leaped fences and scrambled up tall trees, never giving the least thought to being ladylike.

Bronson's peace of mind slowly returned, but he could still be a glum presence. Everyone knew that their home in Still River was, like their time with the Lovejoys, a temporary solution. "Mr. A's inclinations are all for Concord," Abby wrote to her brother Sam.

Emerson was urging them to return to Concord, and while Abby had no desire to go back to a town she saw as dull and unenlightened (apart from their intellectual circle), she understood how positive and profound Emerson's influence could be on Bronson. "I dread his falling into that solitary life he led last summer," she wrote, certain Emerson would "keep a rational view in sight."

In early October 1844, the Alcotts piled themselves and their belongings into a stagecoach and bid Still River a fond farewell. Fred would board with the Alcotts at the new house, but this move was still harrowing for Louisa, who missed her friend Sophia Gardner so much that she was known to walk the sixteen miles from Concord to visit with her. The Alcott girls had formed close attachments in Still River, but at least the family was returning to familiar ground.

Abby's father's estate had been renegotiated, and that income—together with help from Emerson—would buy the Alcotts a house they could at last call home. Edmund Hosmer would take the family in while the search for a suitable dwelling ensued.

Emerson located a 145-year-old house that had once been occupied, Thoreau told them, by a man who believed he would never die. In April 1845, the Alcotts moved in, naming their new homestead "Hillside" after the high slope beyond the house.

Bronson actively turned his back on the world beyond his gates, throwing himself into renovations. His sole labor transformed a neglected property into a rustic showcase, featuring an orchard of two hundred apple and peach trees and a bountiful garden. He built terraces and a piazza with trailing grapevines, and a gurgling fountain within flowerbeds.

Louisa sometimes helped her father weed while he told her the properties and folklore of the herbs he'd planted, and when not tending his modest paradise, he nourished a houseful of young minds. In the evenings, he (or another Alcott) read aloud from Sir Walter Scott, Nathaniel Hawthorne, or Charles Dickens. Louisa especially loved Dickens and dramatized scenes from his books.

Bronson's garden and his children were symbols of rejuvenation and promise. But to Louisa's dismay, he once more opened up their home to others.

Along with Fred Willis, Sophia Foord, a naturalist, came to board with the family and serve as the children's tutor. (Louisa preferred the lofty term "governess.") No sooner had Foord settled in than Charles Lane turned up. He had rejected the Shakers after a year and a half, leaving his son, William, with them. Still in love with the idea of communal life, Bronson had nonetheless vowed to support only his own family; but, for reasons unknown, Abby took pity on her former nemesis and allowed Lane in.

To make himself useful, Lane stuck his nose into the girls' education again, an arrangement that Louisa hated. "More people coming to live with us," she grumped in her journal. "I wish we could be together and no one else."

Lane's chill moralism soaked every joy out of learning, but Louisa had her ways of undermining his diluted authority. When he asked her to list her vices, she logged nine, including willfulness, impudence, pride, and—with a hint of sarcasm— "love of cats."

Charles Lane returned to England in October 1845, after a stay in the US of almost five years. He was never to darken Louisa's schoolroom door again.

* * *

The Alcotts remained committed abolitionists. Like Fruitlands, Hillside was a secret stop on the Underground Railroad, offering fugitives food and rest on the road to freedom. Louisa recorded at least two visitors over the years, including a man she taught to "write on the hearth with charcoal." Bronson and Abby both wrote of harboring "an amiable, intelligent man just 7 weeks from the 'House of Bondage.'" The traveler they knew only as John was "thirty years old," Bronson wrote. John ate meals with the family and gave an "image and a name to the dire entity of slavery."

Louisa was writing as furiously as ever and set up a post office in Concord—like Abby had done at Dove Cottage. Neighborhood friends left letters for one another in a hollowed-out tree stump on a hill between the Alcott house and the neighboring Gowing property.

Clara Gowing, a friend to both Louisa and Anna, described the sisters as inseparable. Louisa took charge, shocking her mild older sister with bold words and deeds, such as taking Clara joyriding in a neighbor's hijacked horse and sleigh. Louisa was a "strange combination of kindness, shyness, and daring," Gowing wrote, "a creature loving and spiteful, full of energy and perseverance, full of fun, with a keen sense of the ludicrous, apt speech and ready wit." She was also moody, Gowing observed, something that was already obvious to Louisa's family and others. "No one could be jollier and more entertaining when geniality was in ascendancy, but if the opposite, let her best friend beware."

Alcott theatricals resumed, and Anna predicted that her younger sister would "write something great one of these days." Far from envious of her sister's talents and outgoing personality, Anna found Louisa "so interesting and funny that other girls seem commonplace." As good an actress as Louisa or better, Anna took the dramatic and sentimental roles while Louisa leaned toward comedy and exaggerated character parts.

One drama the sisters wrote and performed together at Hillside, *Norna, or, The Witch's Curse,* brought such "fame" (as word got around town) that set and costume contributions started rolling in from friends and neighbors: a velvet robe, a plumed hat adorned with silver, long yellow boots, mock pearls, tinsel ornaments. The sisters acted out the entire play, each taking on five or six characters, with rapid changes of dress. One might play a witch, a soldier, and a lady in a single scene.

The Witch's Curse gave Louisa an opportunity to "stalk haughtily upon the stage in the magnificent boots" and called on the girls' ingenuity to rig up a dungeon, a haunted chamber, and a cavern.

Playacting was an acceptable way of expressing thoughts and feelings that might not otherwise see the light of day, and it was a potent outlet for Louisa's writerly imagination.

But as happy as she was acting or writing, she was just as happy outdoors. In a letter, Louisa reported on "a beautiful walk the other day . . . to a pond called Finch pond . . . and now, if you won't laugh, I'll tell you something—all of us waded across it, a great big pond a mile long and half a mile wide, we went splashing along making the fishes run like mad before our big claws, when we got to the other side we had a funny time getting on our shoes and unmentionables, and we came tumbling home wet and muddy; but we were happy." The outing had found them "bawling and singing like crazy folks."

Sophia Foord, who had overseen this outing and often took the girls into the woods to teach them botany, didn't last long as their tutor, ultimately overwhelmed by the ebullience of her charges. She had been lured to her post by Bronson's long-term plan of establishing a village school at Hillside—where he and Foord would share the teaching—but the idea got no support in a community where Bronson was still controversial.

Frustrated when a paid position never materialized, Foord was also unlucky in love: she proposed marriage to Thoreau, who rejected and humiliated her, compounding her unhappiness in Concord. Before she left the Alcott household, she lashed out at Abby, calling the children "indolent" and Bronson and Abby "faulty specimens of parental impotence" because they were so permissive. The Alcotts never replaced her, and for a time, Anna and Louisa attended the local school, making friends with other Concord children.

These years were, Louisa wrote later, "the happiest of my life," with footloose packs of unsupervised children roaming the woods. It was a time when "we had charming playmates in the little Emersons, Channings, and Hawthornes" and "the illustrious parents." Abby and Louisa, who both loved the card game whist, invited neighborhood girls over for evening card parties.

Curious locals traversed the Lexington Road to call on the bohemian Alcotts. Emerson and Margaret Fuller stopped by one day. With the "illustrious" adults clustered by the front door, talk turned—as it often did—to education, and Bronson lamented not having a school to practice his theories in. Fuller replied, "Well, Mr. Alcott, you have been able to carry out your methods in your own family, and I should like to see your model children."

Not a moment later, an ancient wheelbarrow (chariot) appeared outside, steered by Anna, with Louisa up ahead, playing horse, fully harnessed in bit and bridle, and little Abby May decked out as a queen. Lizzie, in the role of dog, barked loudly. "All were shouting and wild with fun, which however, came to a sudden end as we spied the stately group before us." Louisa stumbled, and her sisters rolled into a pile on top of her.

Abby surveyed the heap and gave a brisk wave. "Here are the model children, Miss Fuller."

Louisa imagined herself growing up to be a brilliant and accomplished woman—glamorous, independent, and literary— like Margaret Fuller. In what Louisa would call her "romantic" or "sentimental" phase, she "fell to writing poetry, keeping a heart-journal and wandering by moonlight instead of sleeping quietly."

Surrounded by some of the era's leading intellectuals and activists, men and women who believed in education and the spiritual benefits of literature and the natural world, wild Louisa was never without stimulation. The most stimulating and inspiring of these illustrious adult influences were Bronson's friends Ralph Waldo Emerson and Henry David Thoreau. Both men became Louisa's romantic heroes and, in her writing, thinly disguised love interests, a safe outlet for her passionate imaginings.

Stately Emerson, who appealed to Louisa's teenage idea of what a literary mentor or "master" should be, gave Louisa free rein in his library and enlisted her to tell fairy tales to his daughter Ellen who so much loved Louisa's versions—influenced by the plant and animal stories Thoreau had told on woodland excursions—that Louisa wrote them down for her. A "natural source of stories," Louisa was, and would be "the poet of children," Emerson wrote. "She knows their angels."

One of the books from his library that fired Louisa's imagination, and that was popular in her parents' circle, was *Goethe's Correspondence with a Child*, fictionalized letters between the German author and a young female admirer.

Impressed by the passion of the book's teenage protagonist, Bettine, for her fifty-year-old mentor, Louisa was "at once fired with the desire to be a second Bettine, making my father's friend [Emerson] my Goethe. So I wrote letters to him, but was wise enough never to send them . . . left wildflowers on the doorsteps of my 'Master' . . . [sang] in very bad German under his window, and was fond of wandering by moonlight, or sitting in a cherry-tree at midnight till the owls scared me to bed." Emerson either politely ignored her infatuation or never noticed.

In Thoreau, the man Louisa would later honor in one of her poems as "the genius of the wood," she found the polar opposite of Charles Lane's stern moral instruction. The genius liked his solitude, she knew, but he also liked children, and it must have made her feel special that Thoreau let Louisa and her sisters traipse along as he roamed Walden woods in his straw hat with notebook, pencil, and flute in hand.

Louisa enjoyed and valued her own solitude almost as much as she did congenial company.

In March 1846, for the first time in a household where privacy was a rare commodity, she got to have her own room. "I have at last got the little room I have wanted so long," the thirteen-year-old author pronounced. "It does me good to be alone and mother has made it very pretty and neat for me."

Abby fitted the room out with a needlework basket, a desk by the window, and a closet full of sweet-smelling dried herbs. "I have made a plan for my life," Louisa vowed in her journal, "as I am in my teens, and no more a child. I am old for my age, and don't care much for girl's things. People think I'm wild and queer, but Mother understands and helps me."

Her new room had a door opening into the garden, which would be "very pretty in summer," Louisa wrote, but also an escape. "I can run off to the woods when I like sanctuary."

Abby understood the benefits of letting Louisa loose, to learn from the natural world "what no books can teach." One summer day, Louisa wrote in her journal of taking a solitary run over dewy grass and velvet mosses. It was utterly silent in the woods, and as she watched the sun rise over the meadow, she seemed to see the world with fresh eyes. Something changed in her on that perfect morning, she wrote, and a new faith was born. "I stood there, with no sound but the rustle of the pines, no one near me, and the sun so glorious, as for me alone. It seemed as if I *felt* God as I never did before, and I prayed in my heart that I might keep that happy sense of nearness all my life."

Abby saw not only Louisa's need for sanctuary but her unique nature. "Your temperament is a peculiar one," she wrote to her daughter, "and there are few who can really help you."

But perhaps writing could. Abby told Sam that the process was, for Louisa, "a safety valve to her smothered sorrow, which could otherwise consume her young and tender heart."

For her fourteenth birthday that year, Abby gave Louisa a pen, with a note reading, "May this pen your muse inspire. . . . Believe me you are capable of ranking among the best." (Bronson also supported Louisa's storytelling gifts and gave her a book of her own poems hand-copied in his elegant calligraphic script.) Abby advised Louisa to write when she got sad or angry. "I am sure your life has many fine passages well worth recording, and to me they are always precious. Do write a little each day, dear, if but a line, to show me how bravely you begin the battle, how patiently you wait for the reward sure to come."

Another time, Abby wrote, "MY DEAREST LOUY, I often peep into your diary hoping to see some record of more happy days. Hope and keep busy," she urged, "and in all perplexity or trouble come freely to your MOTHER." Louisa promised to do just that.

With Marmee's help, Louisa came of age at Hillside during those wild, inspired months and years between the spring of 1845 and late 1848, dreaming of love and fame.

The ordeal at Fruitlands had revealed a crack in the family bedrock, a chasm between Louisa's parents, and Bronson's essential ideas hadn't changed. He was still unable or unwilling to provide more than a subsistence living for the pathetic family, and their poverty was now more pressing than ever.

The Alcotts were used to hand-me-down rags and discreet baskets of food left on the doorstop, but in the autumn of 1847, their credit at stores in Concord ran out.

The fact that her father would serenely watch his children go hungry was hard for a skinny, rangy teenager like Louisa to understand. She complained in her diary, "I don't see who is to clothe and feed us, when we are so poor now."

No longer content to sit on the sidelines or dodge creditors—and anxious to keep Hillside from being sold out from under them—Abby defied convention and arranged to find employment.

She already took in sewing, the hallmark of genteel poverty, and it wasn't enough. The family could make ends meet, she decided, only if she and the girls found work, and with few or no employment opportunities available to them in Concord, they would have to fan out.

As a temporary measure, Abby took in a girl boarder roughly Louisa's age. Eliza Stearns was "not insane or dangerous" but "in a state of sad mental imbecility" and had proven too demanding for her family. Her father had resolved to commit her to an asylum, when Abby's cousin Hannah Robie suggested the Alcotts. "I have engaged the care of her for one year, for 4 dollars per week," Abby wrote Sam. Abby hoped that "if by faithful care of this bewildered child we can make her path more . . . straight I shall be well repaid for the sacrifice of personal comfort. I know of no so righteous way of adding to our income and paying our debts."

Around the same time, an invitation arrived for Anna to spend the winter in Walpole, New Hampshire, and open a school there. Anna was sixteen and willing, and Louisa too might have found a teaching position. But Abby argued that Louisa needed "retirement, agreeable occupation, and protective provident care" and was better off at home. Still, more had to be done to provide for the family.

In the spring of 1848, Abby accepted a three-month trial of

a job, for five hundred dollars a year, as matron of a therapeutic water-cure spa, or hot springs, in Waterford, Maine.

Abby set off with Eliza Stearns and seven-year-old May (too young to be left in her father and sisters' care), and wrote often, confiding, "It seems a great experiment in the heart and the life of a family to sever it occasionally; make it bleed at every pore, reunite, heal and live again." She dreamed of them, she said, and agonized over May, eventually summoning Louisa to fetch the family's youngest back to Concord.

By early August, Abby was back home. The experiment had been trying, but after years of anxiety, resentment, and power-lessness, she had proven that she could earn the family's living, even temporarily. She put out word to family and friends that she was seeking a new position in Boston.

The Alcotts hung on at Hillside until the fall of 1848. At three years, this was the longest Louisa and her sisters had ever lived in one house. The decision to leave was "an anxious coun-sel," Louisa wrote. Doomed to part with Concord—and always "preferring action to discussion"—she "took a brisk run over the hill and then settled down for a good 'think' in [her] favorite retreat near an old cart wheel sunk in grass.

"The hopeful heart of fifteen beat warmly under the old red shawl, visions of success gave gray clouds a silver lining, and I said defiantly, shaking my fist at a crow cawing dismally on the fence nearby. 'I will do something, by and by. Don't care what, teach, sew, act, write, anything to help the family; and I'll be rich and famous and happy before I die, see if I won't!'"

The "trials of life began about this time," she later recalled, "and my happy childhood ended."

The Inheritance

Chap 1st

In a green old park where herds of bright
eyed deer lay sleeping under drooping trees & the
clear lake mirrored in its bosom the flowers that
grew upon its edge or clustered round, the graceful
statues placed in cool green nooks, stood
Lord Hamiltons fair & stately home half castle
& half mansion for here & there rose a grey old
tower or ivy covered arch, while the blooming
gardens that lay around it, the light balconies &
tasteful decorations shew that modern skill had
added grace & beauty to the old decaying castle
making it a fair & pleasant home.

The setting sun shone warmly through
the richly stained windows on a group within the
the summer wind blew freshly by lifting the
bright locks of a fair girl who sat weaving
garlands on the vine covered balcony, beside
her stood a young & handsome man, while
just within the shadow of the crimson curtain
a graceful dark eyed lady half reclined
among the pillows of a velvet couch, near
her sat another lady older & more stately whose
proud cold face grew milder as she watched

⇒*9*⇐

"*STICK TO YOUR TEACHING*" *& OTHER DRAMATIC INTERLUDES*

1848-1854

I won't teach; and I can write, and I'll prove it.

—*Louisa May Alcott, journal, 1862*

*T*he Alcotts found a tenant to rent Hillside and left Concord the November that Louisa turned sixteen. As usual, arrangements were made on the fly, and the departure was jarring.

For the next decade, they would be on the move nonstop, living in dreary provisional homes in struggling neighborhoods. (From the time of Louisa's birth until her midtwenties, her family moved more than thirty times.)

Their first stop was a shabby basement apartment on Dedham Street in Boston's crowded South End. After Dedham Street came Groton Street, and after that, grim quarters on High Street, edging one of the worst slums in Boston.

Whatever their address, they were "poor as rats & apparently quite forgotten," Louisa wrote dolefully, "by every one but the Lord."

In the eight years since the Alcotts had fled Boston and their debts, the city had changed dramatically. Back when Louisa had rolled her hoop through the Boston Public Garden, the city had been 95 percent native born and still somewhat agrarian. Now the norm was industrial neighborhoods like the South End, where Louisa lived crowded in among factories and shops, and immigrants made up half of Boston's poor population. Many were Irish, penniless survivors of coffin-ship voyages who didn't have the skills to succeed in the New World.

The wharves where Louisa had once displayed her green shoes to sailors now hosted a teeming shantytown where the homeless shared a single filthy toilet. Only the wealthy had indoor plumbing, so the Alcotts made do with chamber pots and outhouses.

Cholera, tuberculosis, and smallpox were regular visitors, especially in the hot summer months, and the Alcotts were luckier than some; they could board with worried relatives when disease threatened the poorer parts of the city.

On the flip side of Boston's stark poverty was a conspicuous new upper class. Abby had grown up in Boston among wealthy intellectuals committed to the democratic values of the American Revolution: liberty, equality, and justice. The city's new merchant class held commerce and prosperity above ideals, building ostentatious mansions on Beacon Hill and glutting Washington Street with ornate carriages. Shops catered to their lavish tastes. Every window was trimmed with elegant gowns and luxury goods. A dazzling array of concerts, plays, and lectures was available for their entertainment and edification.

Louisa was tormented by the promise of splendor and excitement at every turn. "I try not to covet fine things," she wrote. "It is hard to be cheerful when I think how poor we are, how much worry it is to live, and how many things I long to do I never can."

The bustle and dirt made it hard to think, and she missed the countryside. "Among my hills and woods," Louisa wrote, "I had fine free times alone, and they helped to keep me happy and good, but . . . heaven's so far away in the city, and I so heavy I can't fly up to find it."

Hannah Robie had persuaded a group of rich Bostonians to set Abby up as "a missionary to the poor" at thirty dollars a month, making her one of the nation's first social workers. "I have taken the ship into my own command," she wrote to Sam of her role as breadwinner, "but whether I shall do better as Captain than I have as mate, the revenue and record of the year must decide."

Her mother's activism brought Louisa into contact with Irish immigrant and African American women reduced to bitter toil. Many were illiterate, inspiring Abby—with help from Louisa and sometimes Anna—to offer free evening classes in reading, writing, and arithmetic, enough to help her clients calculate their pay and read bills.

Abby took to her mission with the fierce determination she

brought to every new enterprise. She traversed poor neighborhoods, often with her older daughters in tow, bearing donations of food and clothing. She spoke with mothers about diet and hygiene, and took a special interest in disadvantaged young women—some the same ages as her girls.

Louisa told her diary, "I can't talk to anyone but mother about my troubles and she has so many to bear now I try not to add any more."

Abby too felt the changes keenly, and told Louisa in a note that she longed for "quiet days and simple joys . . . My Diary! Your Diary! Only to think that we neither of us snatch a moment to notch our days! Can they be profitably spent if not a moment can be spared to record the fact that we lived? What is time doing to us?"

Louisa had been plucked from pastoral Concord and set down in one of the meanest corners of urban life, and like her literary idol, Charles Dickens, Louisa would draw on these experiences for her stories. The difference was that she, unlike Dickens, found relief from poverty, since her mother was related to half of Boston's wealthiest inner circle, genteel men and women with little or no clue about—or no interest in looking too closely at—how the Alcotts really lived.

When Anna boarded away from home, as she often did once the family relocated to Boston—working as a nursemaid or governess—it fell to Louisa to keep house alone. "I felt like a caged sea-gull," she wrote." With just three rooms, a kitchen, and a small backyard with no trees to speak of, their basement apartment was beyond cramped, and Louisa had no money to fund distraction or relief.

Everyone else had a place to go to, but solace returned each evening with the faces of her parents and sisters around the table and their lively tales of the city.

After a long dreary day spent scrubbing pots and mopping, narrative was the best consolation Louisa had, and stories of the outside world electrified her.

Bronson's lingering notoriety in Boston still barred him from teaching, but in December 1848, he started up his public conversations again. He had mended with Elizabeth Peabody (who now tutored Lizzie and May, ages thirteen and eight), and he was leasing a room upstairs from Peabody's bookstore on West Street downtown, bringing in a modest income with his conversations.

Though Bronson veered in and out of mental anguish during his family's tenure in Boston, he was as eloquent and intellectually engaged as ever. With Emerson, he formed a society called the Town and Country Club that hosted lectures and kept him in touch with the best minds in liberal New England. Louisa hungrily took in his reports over dinner each night.

The sights and sounds that Abby shared at the table were darker and rooted in compassion; she literally gave needy people the clothes off her back some days, she was so moved by the plight of those she served.

Anna's kindness and patience made her a good match for the work she did, though Louisa worried about her sister as much as she did her mother. When Anna came home to visit, she seemed to Louisa "feeble and homesick," and her anecdotes about nurturing other people's children hovered between their parents' light-and-dark extremes. "I miss her dreadfully," Louisa confessed in her journal, "for [Anna] is my conscience, always true and just and good. She must have a good time in a nice little home of her own some day, as we often plan. But waiting is so *hard*!"

Somehow during the rough winter of 1848, Louisa managed to complete her first story—"The Rival Painters: A Tale of Rome."

Soon after that, she dove into writing her first novel, a Cinderella story (appropriately) that drew with relish on Charlotte Brontë's *Jane Eyre*. *The Inheritance* wouldn't be published in Louisa's lifetime but offered an imaginative escape from the pressures of daily life.

The book's heroine, Edith, a young Italian orphan, lives in

a stately dwelling, half mansion, half castle—a mishmash far from Dedham Street. Edith works as governess to the Hamiltons, a posh English family, in service to the abusive Lady Ida Clare. When a mysterious stranger with the secret to Edith's birth sends word that her father was the long-lost heir to the Hamilton fortune, and also sends a handy copy of the father's will naming her as heiress, proud Edith rips the document to bits and rides off into the sunset with a wealthy young lord instead.

Modeled on the kind of romantic and Gothic novels that Louisa devoured, *The Inheritance* was written in 1849 as an exercise. But like her heroine Edith, Louisa had lived among, and accepted charity from, advantaged relations, friends, and benefactors. Sometimes the Alcotts found themselves welcome as peers and guests; at other times, they were looked down upon or exploited as governesses or teachers, suffering, as Abby put it, "the cold neglect, the crude inferences, the silent reproach of those who profess to love us and desire to help us."

Louisa's tale of hidden worth brims with Alcott values—loyalty, integrity, and family over money and privilege—but it's also about taking a unique stand and trusting your inner compass.

In Boston, she and her sisters also found time to resurrect the Alcott theatricals and performed for family and friends.

The girls handcrafted props and costumes (anything from a harp to glimmering fairy wings) and perfected the art of dialogue, reciting speeches to the word—often Louisa's words. She wrote melodramas such as *The Captive of Castile; Or, the Moorish Maiden's Vow.* Or they performed Shakespeare's plays, giving Louisa a chance to tackle the role of Hamlet with "a gloomy glare and a tragic stalk."

"Anna wants to be an actress, and so do I," she wrote in 1850. A highly unconventional career choice for a young lady of the day, acting satisfied Louisa's love for all things lurid and thrilling, and hinted deliciously of scandal. Writing and a career on the wicked stage were the only occupations that Louisa could imagine for herself. "We could make plenty of money, perhaps," she speculated. "Mother says wait."

Dreamy Louisa was also a practical realist. She saw and accepted reality but had a knack for making the best of it, for entertaining herself and others with her plays, her Hillside mailbox, a family newspaper called the *Olive Leaf,* and many other ventures.

Despite her flourishing creativity, Louisa continued to see her mind as a messy room—and keeping it in order a chore. No matter how hard she tried to sweep away fitful thoughts and moods, they piled up again. Her inner housekeeping was as daunting a task as keeping up with her ceaseless physical chores.

After a long break, she was back to keeping a regular journal again, one that Bronson criticized: while Anna's diary was about others, he noted, Louisa always wrote about herself.

"I don't *talk* about myself," she argued, "yet must always think of the willful, moody girl I try to manage, and in my journal I write of her to see how she gets on."

Louisa's journal was both a way to chart her progress and a dump for frustrations. "Every day is a battle," she confessed at age eighteen, "and I'm so tired I don't want to live; only it's cowardly to die until you have done something."

Bronson called Anna his "peacemaker . . . beloved of all," while Louisa and her futile efforts to be good still frustrated him. Seeing herself through her father's eyes, Louisa could only fail, and judge herself harshly.

Abby recognized the pattern and the pain it caused. Bronson continued to view the alliance between Abby and Louisa as a threat to his authority, but Abby was Louisa's salvation, always on hand with care and sympathy, however burdened her own daily life, always urging her daughter to work out her feelings in writing.

When Abby's social work finally drained her inner resources, her activist brother, Sam, helped her open an "intelligence office" (the employment office of the day) dedicated to finding jobs for the poor—though it must have been obvious to all that the Alcotts were nearly as poor as Abby's clients. Sam had a flyer made up:

> *Best American and Foreign Help. Families, provided at the shortest notice, with accomplished COOKS, good PARLOR and CHAMBER GIRLS, NURSERY MAIDS, SEAM-STRESSES, TOILET WOMEN, and DRESS Makers. Any person paying the subscription of $1 shall be furnished with a ticket, entitling her to a choice of help for six months from Mrs. Alcott's rooms.*

The Alcotts gave of themselves so freely that they sometimes jeopardized their own health and welfare. The whole family contracted smallpox, Louisa reported, from "some poor immigrants whom Mother took into our garden and fed one day." The girls quickly recovered, but Abby's case was more stubborn, and for two weeks, Bronson was unable to leave his bed.

"Father and Mother had no money to give," Louisa observed, "but gave . . . time, sympathy, help."

Louisa understood and sympathized with her mother intensely, writing in 1850, "I often think what a hard life [Mother] has had since she married,—so full of wandering and all sorts of worry! So different from her early easy days, the youngest and most petted of her family. I think she is a very brave, good woman, and my dream is to have a lovely, quiet home for her, with no debts or troubles to burden her. But I'm afraid she will be in heaven before I can do it."

Her mother was her best ally, but Louisa still craved her father's elusive approval. In Bronson, she and her sisters "had the truest of guides and guards," who taught them "the sweet uses of adversity, the value of honest work . . . and the real significance of life."

Not yet fully recovered from his Fruitlands breakdown, Bronson lapsed from time to time into feverish, hallucinogenic thoughts. He wove ideas about the brain, body, magnetism, and stars into a mystical theory, and illustrated with charts and diagrams a manuscript he titled *Tablets*. His writing was done "in a blaze of being," but as before, his genius looked to others a bit like madness. He developed a nagging cough and began to avoid food and sleep again, as at Still River. And while Bronson knew that people judged him for not providing for his family, and called him "heartless and incapable," he could only respond: "So let it seem, but let it not be so."

Afraid that his obsessive preoccupations would overtake him again, Abby shipped her husband off to Concord. It did him good to take morning walks on the hillsides with Thoreau or swim with Emerson in Walden Pond, and he returned to the family with his recovery well under way. "Peace fills his breast," he wrote in a poem at that time.

Louisa slowly began to venture out with her writing. Her poem "Sunlight" was accepted by *Peterson's Magazine* and published in September 1851 under the pen name "Flora Fairfield." A few months later, in May of 1852, the story she had drafted three years earlier, "The Rival Painters," was published in the *Olive Branch,* earning her five dollars.

Driven both by family poverty and by the need and compulsion to create, Louisa was beginning to grasp that she might one day be able to make a living with her pen. Her talent could serve the greater Alcott good. But she was also practical. Unlike her father, Louisa kept an eagle eye on her personal finances—at age eighteen, she began a scrupulous record of her annual earnings— and for now, she needed to diversify.

In 1853, she taught for several months on Suffolk Street. Bronson paid her a visit there, still pining for the classroom himself. Louisa would have gladly handed hers over. The vocation her father loved left her cold, and though necessity drove her back many times, it was never for long.

Louisa also grew attracted around this time to the preaching of the fiery minister Theodore Parker, who had visited Fruitlands and now sometimes attended Bronson's conversations. His advocacy of women's rights resonated deeply with Louisa, and the minister soon joined Emerson and Thoreau among the leading transcendentalists to whom she felt an idealistic, almost romantic attachment.

Parker's unorthodox opinions alienated many Bostonians, and he was forced to preach at the Boston Music Hall instead of a church. His steel-blue eyes gazed intently through gold-rimmed spectacles as he urged his listeners to stand up and fight for social change and abolition.

A public controversy over abolition erupted in April 1851 when a boy named Thomas Sims escaped from slavery in the South, only to be seized and imprisoned in Boston. He was seventeen, younger than Louisa, and she followed his fate with a burning sense of injustice. The federal Fugitive Slave Act of 1850 was under debate at the time in the Supreme Judicial Court of Massachusetts. The law made it illegal to help any enslaved person on the run; fugitives must be returned to enslavement no matter where they were captured, and involvement with the Underground Railroad or other methods of escape made you a criminal. Louisa attended a large rally denouncing the Fugitive Slave Act and dreamed up plots to free Sims before he was sent back. "I shall be horribly ashamed of my country," she wrote, "if this thing happens."

Her father too was absorbed by the crisis, and when the news came, it was grim. Chief Justice Lemuel Shaw upheld the law, and Sims was returned to Savannah, Georgia, where he received a public whipping that almost killed him.

Abby was just as disillusioned at her intelligence office and was fighting exhaustion in her lonely struggles on behalf of the poor. "My life is one of daily protest against the oppression and abuses of Society," she wrote. In an 1851 letter to Sam, she reported helping twenty African American women into "service in the country, where for the present they will be safe. [I] may yet meet the penalties of the [Fugitive Slave] law," Abby wrote. "I am ready."

The horrors of Southern slavery and the pitiful wages and grim conditions faced by immigrants flooding into Boston— another "system of servitude"—enraged and consumed Abby, and Louisa admired the fact that her mother "always did what came to her in the way of duty and charity, and let pride, taste and comfort suffer for love's sake."

Operating the employment service from the Alcott apartment made for a fuzzy line between work and home, and the family's rooms in High Street became "a shelter for lost girls, abused wives, friendless children, and weak or wicked men."

* * *

Louisa longed to pursue her twin callings—acting and writing—but for the moment both remained impractical. Seeking a way to stay busy and useful that winter, she accepted what turned out to be a terrible job in Dedham, a town southwest of Boston.

She was hired as a lady's companion to a "timid mouse" of forty, all wrapped in shawls; but her somewhat sinister employer, Mr. Richardson, soon made it clear that he was the one in search of a companion, not his sister. He kept one room in the dilapidated house—his own parlor—inviting, with a glowing fire and "the balmy breath of hyacinths," and continually called Louisa away from his needy sister. He seemed to expect her to while away long evenings by the fire and be at his beck and call, and Louisa became "a passive bucket, into which he was to pour all manner of philosophic, metaphysical, and sentimental rubbish." Finally—boldly—she spoke up one day and told him she would rather scrub floors than listen to him talk another moment. As revenge, he heaped on other tasks, none of them in her job description, such as oiling his boots.

Louisa withstood her employer's unwholesome attentions for seven weeks, but finally made her quiet way back to Boston on a bleak March day, and when she opened her final wages, she found he had underpaid her.

She was never able to spin this humiliating experience into

comic gold, as she generally did with life's hardships, but in her satire "How I Went Out to Service"—one of many autobiographical stories—her fictional employer, Reverend Josephus, docks her pay, and the Alcott family, indignant, sends the pittance back.

In real life, they probably couldn't afford to.

The following year, one of the Alcotts' old Concord neighbors, novelist Nathaniel Hawthorne, made Bronson an offer.

A string of successful books, including *The Scarlet Letter*, *The House of the Seven Gables*, and *The Blithedale Romance*, had funded the writer's return to Concord after a seven-year absence. Hawthorne would pay the Alcotts fifteen hundred dollars for Hillside, a reasonable if not generous offer. (For Bronson, it was the equivalent of ten years' worth of public conversations.)

The Alcotts accepted, and then rented better lodgings, overextending themselves for a four-story brick house on Pinckney Street—a quiet, narrow cobblestone lane of shuttered town houses—in fashionable Beacon Hill.

Bronson took the sacrifice of Hillside hard. With no base left in Concord, his spiritual center, he planned a lecture tour outside the Northeast. The trip restored his self-esteem and made him feel "important and admired" in a way that he hadn't felt since his visit to Alcott House, the school in England named in his honor. He returned to Boston in February "a half-frozen wanderer" but a changed man, "as serene as ever."

As Louisa told it, the family fed and warmed him by the fire, trying their best not to ask the looming question. Finally, Abby blurted it out: "Well, did people pay you?"

Bronson held up a single dollar bill. "Only that. My overcoat was stolen."

As the girls swallowed back tears, Abby kissed their father. "I call that doing very well. Since you are safely home, dear, we don't ask anything more."

In her embellished version of the story, Louisa claimed that she and Anna took the scene as "a little lesson in real love," but in fact, Louisa could be as critical of her father's shortcomings as he was of hers. An earlier journal entry begins, "Still at High St. Father idle, mother at work in the office, Nan [Louisa's nickname for Anna] & I governessing, Lizzie in the kitchen, Ab doing nothing but grow. Hard times for all."

With the family still very much struggling to get by, Louisa opened a little school for about a dozen children in the Pinckney parlor.

Her students loved her, Abby noted, but Louisa liked teaching less than ever, and in the spring of 1854 she mustered the courage to call on James T. Fields, prestigious publisher of Emerson and the poet Henry Wadsworth Longfellow, with a manuscript under her arm.

She sat restlessly in the great man's office, hemmed in by teetering stacks of books and submissions, while behind a green curtain he read hers—an account of being farmed out for domestic service. The rustle of pages, every cough the great man coughed, every audible breath he breathed, must have been a torment for the ambitious young author.

When Fields emerged, he looked from the pages to her face, and back again. "Stick to your teaching, Miss Alcott," he advised. "You can't write."

The sting of these words might have broken a meeker spirit, but they only riled Louisa. She *did* teach again that summer, but her determination was not to be trifled with.

By fall, she had sold a second short story, "The Rival Prima Donnas," to the *Saturday Evening Gazette,* earning five dollars for the family coffers. It was published on November 11, 1854, under her then pen name "Flora Fairfield."

She also set out that fall to publish her first book. Instead of testing her luck with *The Inheritance,* she revised the little fables she had delighted Ellen Emerson with.

Louisa shared her manuscript with Bronson, who liked it enough to drop it off with Boston publisher George Briggs.

In December, the collected tales were published in book form as *Flower Fables* and earned a small profit. Louisa's take was thirty-eight dollars, a modest sum even then. Only after the thrill of her first big publishing triumph had faded did she consider that she might have requested better terms in her contract. Like her father, she had undersold her mental labor.

At age twenty-two, Louisa boasted in her diary: "Mothers are always foolish over their first-born." She presented a copy of *Flower Fables* to Miss Emerson with pride and was able to stuff a copy into her own mother's Christmas stocking that year. "Whatever beauty or poetry is to be found in my little book," she wrote to Abby, "is owing to your interest in and encourage of all my efforts from the first to last. . . . I hope to pass in time from fairies and fables to men and realities."

As for Bronson, Louisa gave him slippers that Christmas, "to shield the ten philosophical toes," and penned a poem wishing her father a long life, "no matter how empty" his purse might be.

On the heels of publishing her first book, the author found success as an actress and playwright too. Louisa's Boston stage debut, a benefit for the Federal Street Church, where one of her uncles was deacon, was so popular that she was invited to repeat the performance at another location.

Her cousins were showing her off around privileged Boston. Ham and Lu Willis became her first close adult friends, and Ham introduced her to the editor of the *Saturday Evening Gazette*, which gave her access to the popular market for sentimental women's fiction. She would spend the next five years of her career publishing romantic stories in the *Gazette* and other local journals and newspapers, studying literature "markets" and experimenting with writing styles. Her confidence grew as she learned to tailor her lively tales for distinct audiences, from factory and shop girls to ladies of leisure.

Louisa used her winter earnings to buy new trim for her and her sisters' secondhand dresses. She took pride in providing for the family and enjoyed her independence even more. For her next book of stories, *Christmas Elves,* a companion to *Flower Fables,* she asked fifteen-year-old May to draw the illustrations.

Just as Boston was beginning to favor Louisa, the Alcotts' Pinckney Street landlord gave them three months' notice.

The Pathetic Family, observed Louisa, like the hapless Micawbers of Charles Dickens's novel *David Copperfield,* were always looking ahead to better times.

When an offer arrived for the Alcotts to live rent-free for two years in a relative's house in Walpole, New Hampshire, where Anna had taught at age sixteen, the family was in no position to turn the offer down.

Amateur Dramatic Company.

SECOND SEASON---SECOND PERFORMANCE.

TUESDAY EVENING, SEPT. 11, 1855.

Stage Manager,—Miss Louisa Hayward.
Prompter,—Miss Abbie M. Alcott.
New Scenery, by Alfred C. Howland.

THE Company take great pleasure in producing, this Evening, the much admired play, in Two Acts, by J. R. Planche. entitled "The Jacobite." to be followed by the celebrated Farce, "The Two Bonny-Castles," by John Madison Morton.

THE JACOBITE.

Sir Richard Wroughton,	Mr. Alfred Hasmer
Major Murray,	Mr. Henry E. Howland
John Duck.	Mr. Waldo F. Hayward.
Corporal,	Mr. Thomas B. Kittredge.
Servant.	Master Samuel G. Kittredge.
Lady Somerford,	Miss Louisa Hayward.
Widow Pottle,	Miss Louisa M. Alcott.
Patty Pottle,	Miss Annie B. Alcott.

THE TWO BONNYCASTLES.

Mr. Smuggins,	Mr. Waldo F. Hayward.
Mr. John James Johnson,	Mr. Henry E. Howland.
Mr. Bonnycastle, alias Jeremiah Jorund,	Dr. Geo. A. Blake.
Mrs. Bonnycastle.	Miss Louisa M. Alcott.
Helen, (Niece of Mr. Smuggins,)	Miss Annie B. Alcott.
Patty,	Miss Sarah Kittredge.

DOORS OPEN AT 7 .... CURTAIN RISES AT 8.

THE Company return their heartfelt thanks to the public for their liberal patronage, and hope, by increased exertions, to merit a continuance of their favor.

≈10≈

BATTERING RAM

1855–1857

I took my little talent in my hands and forced the world again,
braver than before and wiser for my failures.

—Louisa May Alcott, journal, 1856

*L*ouisa made the move to Walpole a month ahead of the others; she helped out in her cousin Lu Willis's garden and reveled in the good green world of springtime. She got up early in the mornings to run in the pinewoods and watch the sun rise.

When the rest of the Alcotts arrived, Abby relaxed into the relative calm, away from the struggles of Boston for a time. Bronson planted an Alcott garden.

A trendy resort stop in the southwestern part of New Hampshire, Walpole attracted a summer population of rich Bostonians and New Yorkers who sponsored a Shakespeare club and the Walpole Amateur Dramatic Company.

Louisa's early journal entries in Walpole tell of picnics and agreeable neighbors, but her focus soon shifted to the stage as she and Anna threw themselves into Walpole's theater season. The founder of the regional theater took the Alcott sisters under his wing, presenting shy Lizzie with a piano and tapping Anna and Louisa for leading roles all summer long.

Soon they were an essential part of the company, with Anna taking the dramatic roles and Louisa vamping it up in racy character or comedic parts.

Over a three-week season and nine performances, the company entertained audiences of one hundred or more, earning good reviews from as far away as Boston and raking in money for charities (though the Alcott family could have used the income themselves).

But by fall the fun was over. The older Alcott sisters needed to earn a wage to help the family make ends meet, and Walpole offered few options.

Anna took a teaching position at an asylum in Syracuse, and Louisa bravely packed her trunk of homemade clothes and lit out for Boston, determined to shop her new manuscript, *Christmas Elves.*

Bronson warned that it was too late in the season to succeed with a Christmas book, and he was right. She peddled her wares in vain, but there was no turning back. Once in Boston, Louisa would find a means to stay there. Boarding with her cousin Thomas Sewall and his family on Chestnut Street, she took in sewing and worked on a steady stream of stories, determined not to slink home in defeat.

Louisa still couldn't abide disappointing her parents. She wanted them to see her at her best—she wanted to *be* her best—and the need to prove herself to her family and to the world motivated and nourished her.

The day before she turned twenty-three, Louisa wrote a

heartfelt letter home, commemorating Bronson's joint birthday and comparing and contrasting father and daughter. He met hardship with "quiet," Louisa observed; but in her, hardship fueled the fire of resilience. Her spirit and determination would see her through.

In Boston, Louisa made it to the theater at least twice a week, and became a sharp judge of what constituted good acting. She saw that she, like one of her fictional alter egos, Christie Devon, was "no dramatic genius." Her stage talent was only what "any girl possessing a lively fanciful sympathetic nature and ambitious spirit" could muster, and Louisa began to look hard at her long-term options. She "would make a clever actress, never a great one."

As for the short term, needlework was better than teaching. "Sewing won't make my fortune, but I can plan my stories while I work," Louisa wrote, "and then scribble 'em down on Sundays." Scribble she did, and her confidence grew. "I am trying to turn my brains into money by stories," she wrote to her father.

While Louisa toiled in Boston, Abby found good works to do even in affluent Walpole, advocating for one of the town's poorest families, who were living over a cellar that had once housed swine. The landlord had never cleaned the cellar and only obliged when Mrs. Alcott threatened legal action. Two small children in the family were stricken with scarlet fever, and Abby—with sixteen-year-old May and twenty-two-year-old Lizzie in tow—came to their aid, only to learn that (as in the 1850 bout with smallpox) the Alcotts' exposure to disease had placed them in danger. Both girls fell ill, and while May bounced back completely, frail Lizzie did not.

Louisa arrived in New Hampshire that summer of 1856 to find her gentle sister wracked with fever and at death's door.

Committed to homeopathic medicine, the Alcotts didn't call in a traditional doctor, and Louisa and Abby took turns nursing Lizzie back from the brink. It was "an anxious time," Louisa wrote, but when her fragile sister seemed to be on the mend, Louisa worked out plans for returning to Boston. (A winter in Walpole could only be "a nice stupid winter," she predicted, with no plays, lectures, or meetings to speak of.) Bronson, meanwhile, planned a conversational tour of eastern cities.

With some dismay, Abby sent them off. Even before Lizzie's illness, with the family separated, Abby had been lonely and disillusioned with Walpole, "a dark valley of selfish propriety." People there seemed "sent into life to take care of their house, horses, and money. . . . Culture of Soul and Self is no part of the programme." But Lizzie needed care and quiet, and for the time being, Walpole was the best option.

In October 1856, Louisa took a room in Mrs. Reed's boarding-house on Chauncy Street in Boston, a magnet for Boston's best and brightest youth. "[I have] a queer pie shaped room," she wrote Anna, "but nicely carpeted, with two bureaus . . . and a rocking chair for my private benefit."

The city was louder and better than ever, Louisa told her sister, with people "swarming up & down in a state of bustle very agreeable to behold after the still life of Walpole."

Teeming Boston fired Louisa's mind and fueled her principles. She was invited to a state house reception for one of her political idols, Charles Sumner, who had been brutally beaten on the floor of the US Senate after giving an inflammatory anti-slavery speech.

Louisa hunkered down to write. She asked editor William Clapp of the *Saturday Evening Gazette,* a colleague of her cousin Ham Willis, to contract her for a story a month for six months at fifteen or twenty dollars each. Clapp agreed to ten each. But "as money is the principle object of my life just now," Louisa wrote an acquaintance, "I want to add another string or two to my bow." She set to work broadening her market to include higher-paying journals like the *Olive Branch.*

Boston cousins had sewing work for her, and so did Mrs.

Reed, whose attic room, firewood, and food would set Louisa back three dollars a week. If she could wrestle up part-time work as a governess, Louisa calculated, she could make do. Her goal was to spend only the warm months up north with her family.

She was training herself as a businesswoman, taking great pride in her "experiment to be independent of every one but my own two hands & busy head."

Social life was brisk. Happy to have her witty company, Louisa's cousins Lu and Ham Willis often bought her tickets to shows. "I can go in to the Theatre with them all I like & for nothing." Lu had given her a lovely scarlet crepe shawl, and Louisa felt "illuminated" when she put it on.

Never one to ask for assistance, Louisa nonetheless craved it and wished it would materialize on its own. It seemed odd to live in a city "full of very rich relations & yet feel as if I dared not ask them for any help even to find work, for when I do they are so busy about their own affairs that my concerns seem a bother and I go away thinking I will never ask again." Lu and Ham and the Sewalls offered her "something better than money or work, in their good will and sympathy," but she wondered why other wealthy relations didn't reach out and why she felt invisible, considering her mother's family pedigree. Still, Louisa kept an active calendar.

"I think I shall come out all right," she wrote Bronson on

November 29, 1856. "I like the independent feeling, and though not an easy life, it is a free one, and I enjoy it. . . . I will make a battering ram of my head and make a way through this rough-and-tumble world."

Louisa's own wish, she admitted in her journal, was to "prove that though an Alcott I can support myself."

May, seventeen years old and as driven as her older sister, arrived in Boston in November to stay with an aunt who would fund her study at the city's new art school. Louisa saw May as the Alcotts' golden girl, born under a lucky star, and marveled that the youngest Alcott never had to pander. People just seemed compelled to support, or outright fund, her dreams.

Louisa took pride in "sending money home" and helping May, though as things stood, she still wasn't making ends meet. To her relief, the Loverings, parents of former pupils of Louisa's, invited her back to tutor their younger daughter, Alice, three hours a day until the spring. "It is hard work," she admitted in her journal, "but I can do it, and am glad to sit in a large, fine room part of each day."

When she wasn't teaching—or about town with cousins and friends—Louisa sat by the window in her little room at Mrs. Reed's ("which has nothing pretty in it") and wrote feverishly. "I love luxury, but freedom and independence better."

That Christmas of 1856 was the first Louisa spent apart

from her family. After receiving their package in the post, she wrote home, "I clutched it, swept upstairs, and startled the [landlady's] family by dancing a hornpipe with it in my arms, then like a young whirlwind swarmed to my garret, ripped it open and plunged in, laughing crying munching the gingerbread putting on the flannel cap. . . . You dear good souls, to think of me in the middle of your hustle."

The season in Boston hummed with parties and tree trimmings, and brought an avalanche of gifts, including a "handsome silk gown" from her cousin Lu, "the first I ever had," as well as laces, gloves, perfume, and a pretty handkerchief. May turned up at one party, and made Louisa proud. Her younger sister seemed to her "graceful" and "beautifully" behaved. It pleased Louisa to see May admired—and Boston society "astonished that an Alcott should dance and talk like other people."

Anna was stranded in Walpole for the holidays, and Louisa vowed to find her housing in Boston, too—ambitious talk from a twenty-four-year-old with "eight cents in the bank . . . and a fortune in prospect."

By summer of the following year, all the Alcotts reunited in Walpole, with Bronson's mother visiting from rural New York. "A house needs a grandma in it," Louisa decided. Her grandmother's presence was also a revelation—a glimpse into where Bronson "got his nature." Louisa was surprised to learn how active and self-reliant her father had been as a young man and how, like her, his ambitions had been shaped and refined by struggle. "I never realized plainly before how much he has done for himself." She thought of writing a novel based on her father's life and times, with chapters on the Temple School, Fruitlands, Concord, and Boston. "The trials and triumphs of the Pathetic Family would make a capital book, may I live to do it," she wrote.

She was also alarmed to find Lizzie far from recovered. "Betty [Louisa's nickname for Lizzie] was feeble, but seemed to cheer up for a time. The long, cold lonely winter has been too hard for the frail creature, and we were all anxious about her. I fear she may slip away," Louisa confessed, for ethereal Lizzie had "never seemed to care much for this world."

Home was Lizzie's care, and now—with everyone coming and going—it was not the refuge it had been in their childhoods. When Abby brought the patient to the seashore at Swampscott, Massachusetts, that fall, hoping to improve her health, Louisa took the opportunity to slip back to Boston to write and earn money for the family.

Though she worried about Lizzie, wrestled with self-doubt, and collected rejection slips, Louisa was also having the time of her life. She attended preacher Theodore Parker's Sunday evening salons, which attracted leading thinkers and reformers such as Wendell Phillips, William Lloyd Garrison, Julia Ward Howe, and her father's former student Frank Sanborn.

Abby, back in Walpole after her stay at the seashore with Lizzie, anguished over events in the news and longed for a purpose. The political debate over whether Kansas should enter the union as a free state or a slave state had turned Kansas into a battleground—with violence erupting between rival factions—and New England's anti-slavery press hummed with the story.

Cut off from "bleeding Kansas" and the larger struggle for social justice—and weary of her circle in Walpole, which seemed to Abby increasingly oblivious and insensitive—she took to organizing local clothing drives to pass the time. Desperate to lose herself in a good cause, Abby was also desperately worried. Lizzie's lingering symptoms—weight loss, weakness, stomach pains, nausea, vomiting, sweating, hair loss, depression, irritability, drowsiness—seemed to grow worse by the day. Scarlet fever would lead to rheumatic fever (which would ultimately become congestive heart failure).

"The case is a critical one," Bronson wrote. Lizzie seemed to him to have "neither flesh nor strength to spare, and the Eye falling on her wasted form scarcely dares to hope for her continuance."

Before long, the family determined to find a more congenial place for their fading angel. Home meant the world to Lizzie, and Walpole was no home for the Alcotts now. Bronson's thoughts bent again toward Concord, his own spiritual center.

"He is never happy far from Emerson," Louisa understood, "the one true friend who loves and understands and helps him."

Bronson took charge in an uncharacteristically active way, and in September 1857, with Emerson's reliable support, purchased the Moore house and ten acres of orchard right next door to Hillside, the old Alcott house (which Hawthorne had renamed "the Wayside"). The neglected property in the shade of elms and butternut trees was even closer to Emerson's white house than Hillside had been.

Bronson assured Abby that he could "do more for [her], and for myself, from the Concord position than any [other] known to me."

≽II≼

THE
FIRST
BREAK

1857-1859

Give me—for I need it sorely—
Of that courage, wise and sweet,
Which has made the path of duty
Green beneath your willing feet.

—*Louisa May Alcott*, Little Women

*B*ronson renamed the new property, with its many apple trees, "Orchard House," but until it was habitable, they would rent from the Hosmer family again.

Both May and Louisa came home in October, elated with their accomplishments. "I have done what I planned," Louisa wrote, "supported myself, written eight stories, taught four months, earned a hundred dollars and sent money home." She was less enthusiastic about the family's move back to Concord. "The people are kind and friendly, and the old place looks pleasant enough, though I never want to live in it." Louisa called the house "Apple Slump," after a tossed-together dessert. For all the hustle and bustle of relocating, the family understood that they had come back to nurse Lizzie to her end.

Lizzie (whose legal name had been changed to Elizabeth Sewall Alcott during the Alcotts' feud with Elizabeth Peabody, Lizzie's namesake at birth) now became "Betty" in Louisa's journal: "dear Betty a shadow, but sweet and patient as always."

Bronson too described Lizzie as "wasted to the mere shadow of what she was." She seemed hollow, her thoughts bending toward release.

The family made Lizzie the heart of their days, and in part to distract and entertain her, as in the old days, went to work planning and acting in plays. They formed the Concord Dramatic Union with some of Frank Sanborn's pupils (the schoolmaster and radical abolitionist had once been Bronson's pupil). Witty twenty-four-year-old John Pratt was soon smitten with Anna, and Louisa adopted motherless Alf Whitman, who boarded with the Pratts, as her favorite. Besides playacting, they attended skating parties together and rowed on the Concord River.

Louisa teasingly called Alf, who was ten years younger, "my boy."

Though older men such as Emerson and Thoreau peopled her romantic fantasies, Louisa had always—since her days as a confirmed tomboy—longed for a brother, making a point of finding pals she could roughhouse and seek adventure with (or lord over, mother, and play older sister to). And now Alf joined Cy Hosmer and Fred Willis as one of Louisa's surrogate brothers.

In November 1857, Louisa wrote in her journal, "Twenty-five this month. I feel my quarter of a century rather heavy on my shoulders just now. I lead two lives. One seems gay with plays, etc., the other very sad,—in Betty's room; for though she wishes us to act, and loves to see us get ready, the shadow is there, and Mother and I see it." At night, she sat at Lizzie's bedside. "Mother needs rest," Louisa understood, and "Betty says she feels 'strong' when I am near."

Alf Whitman and John Pratt were at the Alcotts' often that winter and the following spring, in the last days of Lizzie's quiet life. Louisa nursed her sister regularly, Alf remembered, excusing herself to climb the stairs and check on Lizzie, but Louisa also kept household spirits up. He saw beneath her dignified front one day when he stopped in after church. "I entered the house without knocking, and as I opened the door of the little sitting-room found Louisa there alone. She had turned her back to the door as she heard me come in and before I could see the garment she was sewing burst into tears and with the words, 'It is Lizzie's shroud,' hurried out of the room."

When Bronson asked Lizzie if she understood that she might not recover, Louisa's Betty replied matter-of-factly. Death, she said, "will be something new in our family, and I can best be spared of the four." To her father, it seemed that she had made her choice.

Everyone knew and accepted that Lizzie was not long with them. They were as mindful and loving as a family could be, but death from congestive heart failure is excruciating. "For two days she suffered much," Louisa wrote near the end, "begging for ether though its effect was gone."

On a mid-March day in 1858, Lizzie set down her sewing needle. It was too heavy, she said. The pain was so bad that she asked to lie in her father's arms and called the others to her side. "All here," she said, and at one point, Louisa saw her eyes open, her gaze piercing in its beauty. "She held our hands and kissed us tenderly," Louisa wrote, but the struggle went on for another day, ending on the night of March 14. Lizzie was twenty-two years old.

"A few moments after the last breath came," Louisa wrote, "as Mother and I sat silently watching the shadow fall on the dear little face, I saw a light mist rise from the body, and float up and vanish in the air. Mother's eyes followed mine, and when I said, 'What did you see?' she described the same light mist."

Louisa and Abby washed and dressed Lizzie's body for burial. "Everything was simple and quiet as she would have liked it," Louisa wrote the next day, along with a poem that named Lizzie "Fittest, to become the Angel."

The family held a private service and sang Lizzie's favorite hymn. "My Emerson, Henry Thoreau . . . and John Pratt carried her out of the old home to the new one at Sleepy Hollow," wrote Louisa, referring to her gentle sister's cemetery plot, "chosen by herself."

"She is well at last," Louisa wrote. "So the first break [in the circle of family] comes, and I know what death means—a liberator for her, a teacher for us."

* * *

The day after the funeral was Anna's twenty-seventh birthday, a reminder that life kept marching. The diminished family shared a solemn breakfast, and Bronson and Abby gave Lizzie's desk to Anna.

A day later, a work crew arrived to start renovations on Orchard House. Lizzie's illness had drawn the family back together, but now they dispersed again. May returned to her studies in Boston, and Anna went to stay with friends. The Hawthornes, who had bought Hillside while still abroad, offered use of Hillside while Bronson and the work crew prepared Orchard House. Temporarily settling into her childhood home—a quieter, sadder place now—Louisa suffered "a lonely month with all the girls gone, and Father and Mother absorbed in the old house, which I don't care about, not liking Concord."

Bronson too drifted in and out of his former study with the distracted air of nostalgia. Work on the new house kept him from brooding too much on the past, but Louisa was not so lucky. Her dreams felt both tantalizingly near and worlds away. "I have plans simmering," she wrote, "but must sweep and dust and wash my dish-pans a while longer till I see my way."

Independent in Boston, she was a writer and an actress. In Concord, she was a spinster at home with her aging parents. Shy, domestic Lizzie had been the likely candidate to care for Bronson and Abby as they grew older—not the brave and ambitious Louisa. Who would oversee the household now? Whose labor would win the family bread?

Three weeks after Lizzie's death, on April 7, Anna announced her engagement, and even Louisa (who vowed never to forgive him for stealing Anna away) had to admit that John Pratt was "a model son and brother—a true man, full of fine possibility."

No one doubted that the lovebirds—both of them shy, fond of acting, and bolder onstage than off—were a grand match. John had been a steadfast presence during the family's agonizing vigil for Lizzie, and his choice as pallbearer hinted at Bronson and Abby's approval. Only the timing was a shock.

For Louisa, the joyous announcement . . . wasn't. It came as a blow, in fact, though she wished the couple real happiness. She had lost Lizzie and would now lose her oldest and dearest confidante and be left to shoulder the family finances and support her parents in their older years.

Fearing depression—her "Slough of Despond"—Louisa spent the summer scheming and combating doubts about her prospects as an author.

When Anna and May came home in June 1858, Louisa hurried off to Boston to visit Lu and Ham Willis, determined to "find interest in something absorbing." Charlotte Cushman's performance as Hamlet left Louisa stage-struck all over again, and she eagerly accepted an offer to play the role of a widow in a new production. "It was all a secret," she wrote—acting was not an entirely respectable occupation for a lady at the time—"and I had hopes of trying a new life, the old one being so changed now." But fate intervened when Mr. Barry broke his leg and shelved the project. "I had to give it up," Louisa wrote, though word of her plans still caused a minor scandal. "The dear respectable relations were horrified by the idea. I'll try again by and by and see if I have the gifts. Perhaps it is acting, not writing, I'm meant for. Nature must have a vent somehow."

For now, she would go where the money was. She had sold another story, and knew she could sell more. The escapist tales and serials she was submitting to the weeklies found a ready audience, but would the work bring in enough income, and would it fulfill her over time?

When the family finally moved into Orchard House that July, Louisa felt restless and out of place, though less deserted with her sisters back home. But Anna was wrapped up in her fiancé and May in her painting. Bronson retreated into his renovation projects. "Now that mother is too tired to be wearied with my moods," Louisa wrote, "I have to manage them alone."

*　*　*

For years, the family had been in motion, hounded by debt, or scattered. Going forward, Orchard House would be a base for the Alcotts for more than two decades.

The house fast filled with visitors curious to see what the family was making of the place. Bronson's handiwork showed in elegant new walkways and gardens, and details such as a clever kitchen drying rack that swung out from the wall to reap the warmth of the hearth.

The girls oversaw the interior decorating, painting and papering both upstairs and down. May claimed panels in "all the nooks and corners" and adorned them with painted birds and flowers. One visitor remembered mottoes scripted in ancient English characters above the open fireplaces. "Owls blink at you and faces peep from the most unexpected places."

Everyone seemed glad to see that the "wandering family is anchoring at last," Louisa wrote. "We won't move again for twenty years if I can help it."

But as soon as her parents were settled at the renovated Orchard House, Louisa made a dash for Boston. "I seem to be the only breadwinner just now," she worried. She boarded with her Sewall cousins on Chestnut Street in Beacon Hill and called on all her old employers. No one had anything for her, and as panic set in and November and her twenty-sixth birthday neared, Louisa began to despair. Lizzie had been set free from earthly care and struggle, so why not her? "Last week was a busy and anxious time, & my courage most gave out," she wrote the family in October 1858, "for everyone was so busy, & cared so little whether I got work or jumped in the river that I thought seriously of doing the latter. In fact did go over to Mill Dam and look at the water."

This matter-of-fact confession hides—but not quite—her true emotional state that day, though Louisa's fictional counterpart in the book *Work* reveals more. Christie Devon, worn down by a string of failed careers, and falsely accused of theft, spots a wedding party with a "bonny bride" on the arm of the bride's father. "Oh, it isn't fair, it isn't right that she should have so much and I so little," Devon laments. "What have I ever done to be so desolate and miserable, and never to find any happiness, no matter how I try to do what seems to be my duty?"

Louisa's character makes her way to Mill Dam and, staring down into the churning water, sees "something white" sweep by. Devon wonders "how a human body would look floating through the night," equating herself with that "phantom" in the water. But before she can act on her fantasy, a hand seizes her, pulling her back to safety.

Louisa recorded nothing of the real-life precedent for this

scene in her journal but hinted at her own inner struggle: "My fit of despair was soon over, for it seemed so cowardly to run away before the battle was over I couldn't do it. So I said firmly, 'There is work for me, and I'll have it, and went home resolved to take Fate by the throat and shake a living out of her.'"

Soon after, Louisa attended a sermon by Theodore Parker on the subject of young women in the labor market. "Don't be too proud to ask," her idol preached, "and accept the humblest work till you can find the task you want." Moved by his timely words, she wrote to him in person, and he advised her during her time of crisis.

Just as she was about to take his advice and accept a dismal sewing position at a reform school far from the city—a situation arranged by her mother's well-meaning cousin Hannah Stevenson—a note arrived. Louisa's former employer Mrs. Lovering wanted to hire Louisa back for another term as Alice's governess. Hannah was "glad and shook hands," when Louisa told her she had found a better offer. Hannah said, "It was a test, my dear, and you stood it."

When Parker heard she had been willing to take the grimmer job, the preacher conceded, "That is a true girl; Louisa will succeed."

But Louisa's stark letter of October—informing her parents that their passionate daughter had looked down from the fifty-foot dam linking Boston to Brookline, with her mind in torment—surely alarmed Bronson and Abby.

They read the letter and called her home.

While Bronson sat shelling beans at the table, they discussed her dreams and plans. He listened. His worry hung on even after the visit ended and Louisa returned to Boston. Six days later he turned up in the city ostensibly on some errand, and stuck close by her side. They took long walks together. Bronson escorted her to dinner and brought her along to lectures and conversations.

In Louisa's darkest hour, Bronson took his daughter— his difficult one, the one who always made light of her own struggles—lovingly under his wing. He treated her as an equal and wrote home that Louisa "bore herself proudly and gave him great pleasure."

Before heading back to Concord, Bronson delivered one of her stories to William Clapp, now editor at the *American Union*.

Soon after her twenty-sixth birthday, Louisa reflected: "This past year has brought us the first death and betrothal—two events that changed my life. I can see these experiences have taken a deep hold." She was wiser, stronger, and surer of herself and her gifts. "I feel as if I could write better now—more truly of things I have felt and therefore know. I hope I shall yet do my great book, for that seems to be my work, and I am growing up to it. I even think of trying *The Atlantic Monthly*. There's ambition for you! If Mr. L. takes the one father carried to him, I shall think I can do something."

"Mr. L." was the writer James Russell Lowell, first editor of the *Atlantic Monthly,* the nation's premier large-circulation literary journal. Bronson, Louisa's champion, had furnished him with a copy of her story "Love and Self-Love."

Profoundly aware of the changes occurring inside her, Louisa understood that "work of head and hand is my salvation whenever disappointment or weariness burden and darken my soul."

Now governessing, writing, and sewing for her supper, busy Louisa sent Anna a list of things that she planned to do with extra earnings to "invest in the Alcott Sinking Fund."

In December 1858, May, now eighteen, returned to the city, eager to continue her studies as an artist. The sisters roomed together on Chestnut Street for a time. "Abby [May] & I are fussing about in Boston," Louisa wrote her friend Alf Whitman. "Abby is at the 'School of Design' & is getting on splendidly, bidding fair to become a second Raphael—She is perfectly wrapped up in drawing skating & dancing."

Preparing for a tour of the West, Bronson wrote asking Louisa to "run up and warm" the house and its "many fireplaces" in his absence. ("Dear man!" Louisa confided to her diary. "How happy he will be if people will only listen to and pay for his wisdom!") He took pride in her enterprise and courage, he said, but as the first Christmas at Orchard House would pass without him, he urged her to stay with her mother as long as possible and make "the house joyous." Louisa agreed, informing Alf Whitman, "I am spending my Christmas in Concord to help with some little jollifications."

Louisa had no sooner made it back to the city after the holidays than Abby became seriously ill. The worried daughter hurried back to Orchard House to help Anna care for their mother, and mused in her journal, "Wonder if I ought not to be a nurse, as I seem to have a gift for it. . . . If I couldn't write or act I'd try it. May yet."

When Bronson returned from his tour, Louisa slipped back to Boston and kept busy teaching, writing, sewing, and soaking in the benefits of lectures, books, and stimulating company. "Won't teach any more if I can help it; don't like it; and if I can get writing enough can do much better."

Louisa had already earned more that year—her third year of independence—than she had hoped or expected to: "Supported myself, helped May, and sent something home." She had done it all without borrowing "a penny, and [had] only five dollars given me. So my third campaign ends well."

≫12≪

BOILING OVER

1859–1860

*To and fro, like a wild creature in its cage, paced that
handsome woman, with bent head, locked hands, and restless
steps. Some mental storm, swift and sudden as a tempest
of the tropics, had swept over her.*

—Louisa May Alcott, "Pauline's Passion and Punishment"

*F*or most of Louisa's lifetime, the Alcott intellectual and transcendentalist circle were at the forefront of abolitionist New England. But three decades of peaceful protest against slavery had led nowhere, and Emerson, Thoreau, and Bronson, among many others, had come to believe that two wrongs would (and must) make a right. Violence against the injustice of slavery was both justifiable and inevitable.

Bronson's former student Frank Sanborn—now Concord's schoolmaster; a committed activist; and a member of the Secret Six, a covert committee organized to raise money to support the militant reformer Captain John Brown—would bring Brown to Concord for a day.

Brown, a fierce anti-slavery advocate, would speak at town hall on May 8, 1859, and word of the rally set Concord buzzing. Brown's reputation preceded him, and no one doubted that his high motives would eventually lead to more bloodshed.

Back in May 1856, a mob of hundreds of pro-slavery Missourians had crossed the border into Kansas and attacked the free-soil stronghold of Lawrence, looting homes and shops, torching the Free State Hotel, and trashing newspaper offices.

Furious over the attack—and the subsequent caning of progressive senator Charles Sumner on the floor of the Senate after Sumner's incendiary speech denouncing pro-slavery politicians—John Brown had taken matters into his own hands. "These men are all talk," he'd said of the organized abolitionist movement. "What we need is action—action!"

Brown had plotted revenge. He and his sons had kidnapped five pro-slavery men from their homes near Pottawatomie Creek, Kansas, and executed them with broadswords. Two years later, Brown and his followers had gunned down a slaveholder, freed eleven African Americans, and escorted the slaves north to Canada.

Brown addressed those at the Concord town hall with fiery rhetoric, and worshipful transcendentalists cheered him as a warrior for good. Bronson (who at Fruitlands had refused to rob a sheep of its wool) proudly shook his new hero's hand and pasted a picture of Brown into his journal. Emerson supported Brown too, and Thoreau called his violent activism in frontier Kansas "the public practice of humanity."

Five months later, convinced that an ongoing campaign of abolitionist violence would collapse the institution of slavery once and for all, Brown made a midnight raid on the

United States Armory in Harpers Ferry, Virginia (now in West Virginia). He intended to seize the armory's supplies—nearly ten thousand muskets and rifles—and to arm slaves on neighboring plantations, but the revolt he envisioned, which he hoped would prompt a collapse of slavery in the United States, never took place. Brown had seized the armory but, without help, couldn't defend it. His October 16 campaign was crushed days later by US Marines led by Colonel Robert E. Lee.

Half of Brown's conspirators were killed in the struggle, along with two of his sons. Brown, his surviving sons, and three others were seized and imprisoned.

News of the raid broke over the national telegraph wire, spread like wildfire, and left Concord in an uproar.

"We are boiling over with excitement here," Louisa wrote to Alf Whitman in early November. "We have a daily stampede for papers, and a nightly indignation meeting on the wickedness of our country and the cowardice of the human race. I'm afraid mother will die of spontaneous combustion if things are not set right soon."

But things were not sct right.

Thoreau, who avoided public life whenever possible, wrote and delivered a heartfelt defense of the raid to both Concord and Boston audiences. "I am here to plead [Brown's] cause with you," he told them. "I plead not for his life, but for his character,—his immortal life." But John Brown was found guilty of treason, murder, and insurrection and was executed on December 2, 1859. "A meeting at the hall," Louisa recorded in her journal, "and all Concord was there. Emerson, Thoreau, Father, and [Frank] Sanborn spoke, and all were full of reverence and admiration for the martyr."

Rumors of war between the North and South had young men from several military units clustered in the Great State Encampment near Concord to carry out drills. "Town full of soldiers, with military fuss and feathers," Louisa wrote in her journal, bemoaning that, as a woman, she couldn't participate. "I like a camp, and long for a war to see how it all seems. I can't fight, but I can nurse."

The poem "With a Rose, That Bloomed on the Day of John Brown's Martyrdom," written by Louisa in honor of her fallen hero, was published the following January in the *Liberator*. That acceptance came shortly after James Russell Lowell, editor of the prestigious *Atlantic*, bought Louisa's story "Love and Self-Love."

"I felt much set up," she wrote in her journal. "And my fifty dollars will be very happy money. People seem to think it is a great thing to get into the *Atlantic*." She saw this acceptance as a turning point, as did her parents, both of whom noted the triumph in their journals. "I've not been pegging away all these years in vain," wrote Louisa, "and may yet have books and publishers and a fortune of my own. Success has gone to my head, and I wander a little. Twenty-seven years old and very happy."

The anti-slavery journal *Commonwealth* soon bought "M.L.," a daring tale of interracial marriage that the *Atlantic* had rejected, and when Louisa sent Lowell a new story called "A Modern Cinderella" in April 1860, he snatched it up for the *Atlantic*'s October issue.

The Alcotts hosted a reception at Orchard House that spring for John Brown's widow and her widowed daughter-in-law. Five months had passed since Brown's execution, and while only select friends and supporters had been invited to attend the event, word spread fast, and well-wishers and curiosity seekers turned up in droves. Louisa spent the day running platters of sandwiches and pitchers of tea from kitchen to parlor, noting the plainspoken widow's "natural dignity."

That same week, after Anna's two-year engagement to John Pratt, "The dear girl was married on the 23rd," Louisa wrote at the end of May 1860. Anna's wedding took place on "the same day as Mother's" thirty years before, and guests included Elizabeth Palmer Peabody (the feud long forgotten), Thoreau, Frank Sanborn, and the Emersons. (Louisa envied Anna when "Mr.

Emerson" kissed her. "That honor would make even matrimony endurable," she wrote, "for he is the god of my idolatry, and has been for years.")

The ceremony was performed by Abby's brother, the Reverend Sam May, in the front parlor "with no fuss, but much love, and we all stood round her." The orchard was bright with blossoms, and Anna's hair was adorned with lilies of the valley, John's favorite flower. Louisa and May wore gray and held roses. In her journal, Louisa called her own wedding attire "sackcloth . . . and ashes of roses; for I mourn the loss of my Nan [Louisa's nickname for Anna] and am not comforted." She had still not forgiven her affable new brother-in-law for spiriting Anna away.

After a small feast on the front lawn "under our Revolutionary Elm," Thoreau played a German folk tune on his flute, and the "old folks" danced in a circle around the couple, "a pretty picture to remember," Louisa admitted. It was a day of love, friendship, and spring flowers—a joyful day, but Louisa could not (or not quite) feel joy, at least for herself. She disguised with brave jokes her sorrow over what she saw as the loss of Lizzie and Anna. Before the guests had arrived, Abby had found her "putting a small wreath of wood violets around a picture of Lizzie that hung in the parlor." Louisa looked up tearfully at her mother and quipped, "I am trying to keep Lizzie's memory inviolate."

She wrote Anna days later to describe the "bereaved family" struggling on without big sister, "washing dishes for two hours and boiling the remains of the funeral baked meats."

Louisa had a suitor of her own that spring, a Southern gentleman she met on a train who, when she refused his advances, insisted on "haunt[ing] the [Lexington] road with his hat off." He blitzed her with letters, but the family chased him off, and peace was restored. Thanks to Abby's mindful intervention, Louisa also turned down a marriage proposal from a Mr. Condit, a man in a position to assist the Alcott family financially. Grateful "the wise mother" saved her from the "impulse to self-sacrifice," Louisa penned a curt reply to her suitor: "I have decided it would be best for me not to accept your proposal. In haste, L.M. Alcott."

Weeks later, Louisa paid Anna a call at her new cottage in Chelsea, across the river from Boston, "where she and her mate live like a pair of turtle doves." The visit didn't change Louisa's mind about marriage. "I'd rather be a free spinster," Louisa admitted, "and paddle my own canoe."

In June, she attended a Boston service for her friend Theodore Parker, who had died of tuberculosis in Florence, Italy. "Music Hall was full of flowers and sunshine, and hundreds of faces, both sad and proud. . . . I was very glad to have known so good a man, and been called friend by him." Apart from Emerson and Thoreau, there was no one outside her family that Louisa had respected more.

The Hawthornes returned from Europe that July, and the Alcotts' exotic neighbors gave the family something to talk about besides political news. "Mr. H is as queer as ever," Louisa reported in her journal, "a mysterious looking man in a big hat and red slippers darting over the hills or skimming by as if he expected the house of Alcott were about to rush out and clutch him."

Nathaniel Hawthorne was both famous *and* famously shy and reclusive. He especially avoided Bronson, who loved to chat and whose politics conflicted with Hawthorne's own more conservative views. Hawthorne's wife, Sophia (formerly Sophia Peabody, Elizabeth Peabody's sister), also kept a reasonable distance, given her history with Bronson and the failed Temple School.

Though Louisa later fondly remembered wild summer days spent swimming with May and the Hawthorne and Emerson children in Walden Pond, she had little abiding interest in the Hawthorne daughters—pretty young Rose, or Una, a teenager who seemed to care for nothing but horseback riding. It was their brother, Julian, whom Louisa favored, "a worthy boy full of pictures, fishing rods and fun." Excepting her sisters, she had always liked boys best.

Julian would afterward recall Louisa as a born leader with a keen sense of humor (how she'd sprung from earnest Bronson, whom the Hawthornes mocked, Julian couldn't imagine), though it puzzled him that such a passionate person, fourteen years his senior, had never fallen in love (at least not publicly).

Neighborhood distractions aside, by August, Louisa was writing at white heat—and was as rare a sighting on the Lexington Road as peculiar Mr. Hawthorne. She was hard at work on *Moods,* her long-planned literary novel, and was never one to tread lightly into a new project.

For Louisa, the creative process was a blissful whirlwind or "vortex," one she gave herself up to completely. The worlds and people she imagined eclipsed and became more real to her than the world at hand. She lost sight of the time, the weather, even the need to eat or sleep. Her fits usually lasted only one or two weeks, and "she could find no peace" until the work was through and she emerged "hungry, sleepy, cross, or despondent."

The lamp burned late in the second-story window of Orchard House during those summer nights, and Louisa's family knew enough to leave her to it. "Genius burned so fiercely that for four weeks I wrote all day and planned nearly all night, being quite possessed by my work. I was perfectly happy and seemed to have no wants."

Louisa had created a protagonist in her own youthful image.

The impetuous Sylvia Yule of *Moods* struggles to control her emotions and curb impulses. She agonizes over her feelings for rival admirers Adam Warwick and Geoffrey Moor, modeled on Louisa's own early love interests, Thoreau and Emerson, and depicts an ambitious young woman with no place in conventional society.

With the creative fever passed, Louisa set the manuscript aside to ripen. "Daresay nothing will come of it," she wrote in her journal, "but it had to be done."

Weeks later, she plucked up the courage to read her draft aloud to Anna during a visit, who encouraged her. But Louisa's time seemed to be swallowed up by housework and tedious visitors. Even worse, May would escape Concord that month to teach art and live with their uncle Sam in Syracuse, leaving Louisa alone with her parents again.

"What shall I do without her?" Louisa wrote to Anna. "Her room is so empty and the house so old and still without our lively girl."

In her journal, Louisa was more candid, even bitter. May was "one of the fortunate ones" who got what she wanted easily. "I have to grub for my help or go without," Louisa grumped.

Word came that the *Atlantic* would publish a third story, "Debby's Debut," but the impatient author couldn't help but brood. Lu Willis had invited Louisa up to New Hampshire for a visit, "very aggravating to a young woman with one dollar, no bonnet, half a gown, and a discontented mind."

That December, she again complained of having no decent gown to wear to an anniversary observance for John Brown. Instead she sent a poem that she deemed unworthy. "I'm a better patriot than poet."

At age twenty-eight, she felt dreary, old, and restless.

"She is not wanting in Talent and Character," Bronson wrote to his mother, perhaps sensing Louisa's suffocating need for independence and movement. "I see nothing to prevent her becoming a favorite with the public, as she becomes generally known. Her mother hopes good things of her, in which hope her father certainly joins."

Louisa's journal wrapped up the year 1860 with resigned melancholy: "A quiet Christmas, no presents but apples and flowers. No merry making for Nan and May were gone, and Betty under the snow. But we are used to hard times, and as Mother says, 'While there is famine in Kansas we mustn't ask for sugar plums.'"

❦ 13 ❦

OWLING

1861–1863

Being fond of the night side of nature, I was soon promoted to the post of night nurse. . . . I read their lives in the night.
—*Louisa May Alcott*, Hospital Sketches

*T*he year that opened the bloodiest chapter of American history began quietly at Orchard House. Louisa scribbled away upstairs, working out a gritty autobiographical novel called *Success,* while Bronson delivered bottles of home-brewed hard cider to the neighbors.

But when Abby came down with her (now regular) winter illness that January of 1861, "I corked up my inkstand," Louisa wrote, "and turned nurse."

She returned to her writing desk in February, but it wasn't *Success* she picked up. It was her earlier effort, *Moods.*

Nothing else Louisa ever wrote absorbed her quite like this novel. The previous August, the project had "possessed" her, and when she descended into her vortex again on February 2, she stayed there twenty-three days, rarely pausing to sleep or eat. Apart from a daily run on the quiet roads at dusk, she almost never left her desk.

Bronson broke from his own writing in the downstairs study to deliver "his reddest apples and hardest cider for [Louisa's] Pegasus to feed upon." Her passionate absorption was both familiar and agreeable to him, and her "dashes of wit and amusement," when she did emerge, stirred "us chimney corner ancients."

Abby ventured in and out of Louisa's room with "cordial" cups of tea, pleading with Louisa to stop and eat, but in vain. Picking up on her daughter's energy, Abby made a creative contribution of her own. "Mother made me a green silk cap with a red bow, to match the old green and red party wrap, which I wore as a 'glory cloak.'"

Louisa's thinking cap served its purpose. "After three weeks of it," she wrote, "I found that my mind was too rampant for my body, as my head was dizzy, legs shaky, and no sleep would come. So I dropped the pen, and took long walks, cold baths, and had Nan up to frolic with me." The role of family genius suited Louisa well. Doted on and fussed over by her family, she was in her element.

Moods never altogether satisfied her, but Louisa set down her pen with a sigh of relief on February 25, 1861, assembled her parents and Anna, and read the fruits of her labor aloud.

"Emerson must see this," her father said.

Louisa was stunned and pleased. "I had a good time," she wrote in her journal, "even if it never comes to anything, for it was worth something to have my three dearest sit up till midnight listening with wide-open eyes to Lu's first novel." Her book had made her loved ones laugh and cry, but the nagging doubt remained. "They are no judges."

Nearly every publisher in Boston judged that *Moods* should

be shortened. One demanded "a story that touches and moves me . . . a story of constant action, bustle and motion. What will the characters *do*?"

Disenchanted, Louisa tossed her pile of pages into a spidery cabinet and vowed to leave it there.

All that winter and spring, Louisa restlessly followed national news. The previous December, South Carolina had seceded from the union; in the months since, ten more states had followed suit. War was imminent. Despite Louisa's distraction, her own stories clamored, "demanding to be written," but Louisa "let them simmer." The longer they were "bottled up," she knew, "the better it would be."

But her plan to catch up on household duties and then dive back into writing was foiled when John Brown's daughters Annie and Sarah arrived to board for a time with the Alcotts. Abby needed Louisa's help keeping house. "I think disappointment must be good for me," the thwarted author quipped, "I get so much of it; and the constant thumping Fate gives me may be a mellowing process; so I shall be a ripe and sweet old pippin before I die."

* * *

When war finally came, on April 12, 1861, Bronson declared in his journal that it was abolition's finest day. The Concord town common was suddenly thick with boys in blue coats, clumsy recruits led by inexperienced sergeants, and everyone trying to puzzle out their roles. Louisa took it all in, bemused. The new enlistees made up for in spirit what they lacked in skill. They "poke each other's eyes out," she wrote, "bang their heads & blow themselves up with gunpowder most valiantly."

Louisa herself wanted nothing more than to "fly at somebody," but the tension softened her too: "In a little town like this we all seem like family at times like these."

In the blink of an eye, the young men began to vanish, headed for what most believed would be a short stint of glory, a summer of adventure. Emerson's son Edward organized a unit called the Concord Cadets. Abby and Louisa joined three hundred other Concord women for a two-day marathon in town hall, "sewing violently on patriotic blue shirts."

Stranded at Orchard House, Louisa "wrote, read, sewed and wanted something to do." In the spirit of readiness, she pored over a medical treatise on gunshot wounds, still contemplating a position as army nurse. "There is no opening for me at present," she wrote to Alf Whitman.

During the first winter of the war, finances forced Louisa back to teaching; Elizabeth Peabody brought her on to run a kindergarten at the Warren Street Chapel in Boston. The distinguished James T. Fields, who had once advised Louisa to stick to her teaching (and now published her writing in the *Atlantic*), offered forty dollars to help her set up her classroom.

Fields and his second wife, Annie, who was Louisa's distant cousin, also invited the young writer to board with them. Their Greek revival mansion overlooking the Charles River functioned as a salon, and the Fields hosted a steady stream of literary luminaries.

Living "in style in a very smart house with very clever people" inspired Louisa. The guests at the salon were a breed apart from the threadbare intellectuals she knew in Concord. These writers—the likes of Henry Wadsworth Longfellow, Oliver Wendell Holmes Sr., and Harriet Beecher Stowe— were as popular as they were esteemed. All had made successful careers from their art.

Louisa enjoyed the company but also resented playing the performing seal alongside her beautiful cousin. Annie was just a year older than Louisa and a clever, fashionable hostess. "Hate to visit people who ask me to help amuse others," she complained in her journal. "What [a] false position poverty can push one into."

Bronson doubted that Louisa's heart was in teaching, and he was right. She couldn't even fake it. By the end of March she was losing money, commuting thirty miles between Concord and Boston to avoid the salon. Finally she convinced May to finish out the school year for her, and Louisa churned out a story that earned her thirty dollars, the equivalent of four months' teaching salary but not enough to repay Fields.

"A wasted winter and a debt of 40$," she grumped, "to be paid if I sell my hair to do it."

A pacifist at heart whose philosophies seemed, just now, irrelevant, Bronson found no direct way to support the war effort. He kept up with the news, following every battle "with an avidity unknown before," and ached for each Union defeat. Thoreau's house was a magnet for him in that dark season. Wrestling a stubborn case of bronchitis, Thoreau had ignored medical advice to rest in a warm climate and had been failing since winter. He had contracted tuberculosis and was in a swift decline, too weak since September to visit his beloved Walden Pond; his journal had ended abruptly in November.

Bronson had visited the night of New Year's Day 1862, and had been sad to find his friend "failing and feeble."

When Thoreau died, on May 6, 1862, Bronson was picked to read at his service, which both Louisa and Anna attended. At Emerson's request, the funeral was a public burial from church, something "Henry would not have liked," Louisa wrote, "but Emerson said his sorrow was so great he wanted all the world to mourn with him." She sent word to Sophia Foord (despite Thoreau's cruel rejection of Foord's marriage proposal years before, she had asked to be notified), along with a clipping of andromeda, his favorite plant, from a wreath that the Alcotts had placed on his coffin.

Louisa processed the loss quietly, keeping busy with her stories. She said men like Thoreau "never seem lost to me but nearer and dearer for the solemn change." She could not yet mourn a life that was still so present for her. But knowing that Thoreau was no longer in Concord gave her one less reason to want to be there herself.

Around the same time, Louisa attended a reception for the writer Rebecca Harding (later Davis), who had hit gold with her popular muckraking novel *Life in the Iron Mills*. Louisa admired Harding's writing, and Harding noticed Louisa even before they spoke that night: "I saw . . . a tall, thin young woman standing alone in a corner. She was plainly dressed, and had that watchful defiant air with which the woman whose youth is slipping away is apt to face the world which has offered no place to her."

When Louisa introduced herself, she didn't mince words: "These people may say pleasant things to you, but not one of them would have gone to Concord and back to see you, as I did."

In her journal, Louisa described meeting Harding, who said "she never had any troubles, though she writes about woes. I told her I had had lots of troubles, so I write jolly tales, and we wondered why we each did so."

Many of the tales Louisa wrote throughout that summer found eager homes with popular weeklies such as *Frank Leslie's Illustrated News*. She submitted a long story called "Pauline's Passion and Punishment" to a contest sponsored by Frank Leslie, in the hopes of winning the one-hundred-dollar prize.

In a June letter to old pal Alf Whitman in Kansas, Louisa wrote, "I intend to illuminate the *Ledger* with a blood & thunder tale as they are easy to 'compoze' & are better paid than the moral & elaborate works of Shakespeare, so don't be shocked if send you a paper . . . [with a] title like this 'The Maniac Bride' or the 'Bath of Blood. A thrilling tale of passion.'"

The weeklies not only paid a whole lot better than the *Saturday Evening Gazette*, but they boasted wider circulation. Louisa's blood-and-thunder tales were devoured by an avid national readership hungry for the sensational.

But commercial success wasn't her only reward for writing pulp fiction. Published anonymously or under a pen name, Louisa's "rubbishy" tales allowed her to let it rip. She got to tackle taboo subjects such as interracial love, or melodramatic themes of lust and betrayal, murder and revenge, often in exotic settings. She got to duck out of respectability for a while and inhabit the world of scheming heroines and villainous lovers. Her blood-and-thunder plots let her plumb her characters' darkness and track them in psychologically complex ways.

Louisa kept these assignments—"that class of light literature in which the passions have a holiday"—a secret all her life. For one thing, they would have harmed her reputation as a children's writer, established with *Flower Fables*.

She also kept them quiet out of respect for her family and their elevated circle. What would her father make of his Louy writing thrillers? Despite espousing progressive social and political ideals, Concord was a small town with high standards. "To have had Mr. Emerson for an intellectual god all one's life," Louisa confessed in her journal, "is to be invested with a chain armor of propriety."

In an interview later in life, she confessed, "I think my natural inclination is for the lurid style. I indulge in gorgeous fantasies and wish that I dared inscribe them upon my pages and set them before the public."

By 1862, Louisa had already been a professional writer for a decade with fairy tales, poetry, literary fiction, and many styles of popular fiction under her belt; what's more, she had learned a trade and supported herself, which even prestigious authors such as Hawthorne struggled to do.

By November, the Civil War had been raging for nearly two years, with Louisa sewing bandages on the sidelines. "I long to be a man," she wrote, "but as I can't fight, I will content myself with working for those who can."

But she wasn't content. Lizzie was gone; May was living a free, happy life as an artist; Anna and her husband, John, were expecting their first child; the illustrious parents were getting old.

With her own thirtieth birthday fast approaching, Louisa (who joked she was a spinster long before she was one, by the standards of her day) felt on edge, desperate for adventure before it was too late. She needed to let out her "pent-up energy in some new way," and since thirty was the minimum age for being an army nurse, her thoughts bent back in that direction.

After the July 1861 Battle of Bull Run, the first major conflict of the war, Dorothea Dix—formerly an assistant at Bronson's Temple School and now superintendent of army nurses—had been forced to slacken her strict rule that only plain, married matrons of a certain age could volunteer. The army had since admitted *any* respectable woman of age willing to risk life and limb in its hospitals. An application and recommendations were still required, and Louisa sent in her name through her mother's cousin Hannah Stevenson in November.

"I want new experiences," Louisa wrote, "and I am sure to get 'em if I go." She would also, for the first time, be truly independent of her family, able to challenge herself without her mother's emotional protection or her father's gentle criticism.

While she read medical treatises and awaited her call to duty, Louisa put her scant wardrobe in order ("Nurses don't need nice things, thank Heaven!") and dashed off tales and letters. She sent Concord nuts and apples to male friends serving on the front lines, told them her plans, and joked, "If you intend to be smashed in any way, just put it off till I get to Washington to mend you up."

Orders came on the morning of December 11, 1862. She was to report to the Union Hotel Hospital in Georgetown at once. "I was ready," wrote Louisa, "and when my commander said 'March!' I marched."

Meanwhile, the new commander of Abraham Lincoln's Union Army of the Potomac, Ambrose Burnside, had tried to sneak in a pre-winter strike against Robert E. Lee's Confederate Army of Northern Virginia. On the day that Louisa received her orders, Burnside's engineers were constructing pontoon bridges over the Rappahannock River, with troops poised to cross into Fredericksburg, which had been evacuated.

Abby, pregnant Anna, and May—back home from Syracuse—helped fill Louisa's luggage with traces of home. In the rush and bustle, someone made tea but added salt instead of sugar. "I have a confused recollection of . . . my family swarming after me," Louisa wrote, "all working, talking, prophesying and lamenting, while I packed."

Conscious that she might not see her family again, she kept up a bold front until the last minute, when everyone else broke down with her. "Shall I stay?" she asked Abby.

"No," her mother reassured. "Go! And the Lord be with you."

"Shall I ever see that dear old face again?" she wondered on the doorstep.

Abby's fluttering wet handkerchief was Louisa's last glimpse of Orchard House for a while.

As Louisa "set forth in the December twilight," escorted by Julian Hawthorne and her sister May, Louisa felt like "the son of the house going to war." Because he was traveling at the time, Bronson missed her hasty send-off, but he too joked to friends (with uneasy pride; Louisa was reporting to war in perilous times) that he was sending his only son to war.

Louisa spent a last civilian evening in Boston with her cousin Lizzie Wells, and the next day had a tooth filled. She procured warm clothes from a friend, a cash gift from the Sewalls, and a new traveling veil. She hunted down the official who could authorize her volunteer ticket, met Anna and John for dinner, and after another weepy farewell at the train station, set out "full of hope and sorrow, courage and plans." That same day, though she might not have been aware of it, Union soldiers looted Fredericksburg, smashing china and destroying furniture.

As the day dimmed and the landscape beyond the train window changed from urban to rural, Louisa chatted with her seatmate from time to time to ease the loneliness. While her train chugged south through the night, bluecoats were dragging pianos into the streets of Fredericksburg, pounding out wild patriotic tunes while their officers anguished over Confederate strategy. Could Burnside's plan lead to victory?

The train didn't deliver Louisa directly to Washington. In New London, Connecticut, she changed to a steamer, which ferried her through the night to New Jersey. An inexperienced traveler, she wryly supposed the ship would "blow up, spring a leak, catch fire, or be run into . . . [all] because I'm here to fulfill my destiny."

In Jersey City, she climbed aboard a train bound for Washington. As it chugged through Pennsylvania and Maryland, Burnside was pointing fourteen brigades up a hillside known as Marye's Heights.

Behind a stone wall near the crest of the hillside, a branch of Lee's army crouched in wait.

Not one Union soldier made it within thirty yards of the

wall once the rebels opened fire. The air filled with smoke and thunder, and a Union commander watched his men seem to melt "like snow coming down on warm ground."

Louisa arrived in wartime Washington at night. As she passed through the city, her hired driver pointed out the unfinished Capitol dome and the illuminated White House with carriages "rolling in and out of the great gate."

The Union Hotel had been hastily converted to a hospital. The place Louisa would call "The Hurly-burly House" was poorly lit, overpopulated, and (because many of its windows were nailed shut) not well ventilated. Some windowpanes had been smashed, which only served to let in the cold, and there was a "trying quantity of men lounging about" when Louisa arrived. "It struck me that I was very far from home."

Mrs. Hannah Ropes, the hospital matron, greeted her, and wrote that night in her journal, "We are cheered by the arrival of Miss Alcott from Concord, the prospect of a really good nurse, a gentlewoman who can do more than merely keep the patients from falling out of bed."

As Louisa crawled under her blankets that night, the frosty air on the steep plain above Fredericksburg rang with agonized cries.

It took four days for the first wounded to arrive in Georgetown from Fredericksburg, and by then, Louisa already had her hands full with "pneumonia on one side, diphtheria on the other, and five typhoids on the opposite." Antietam, the bloodiest clash of the war to date, had filled the hospital three months earlier, and many beds were still claimed.

On the morning of December 17, a boy stepped into the hospital to shout the news. The Fredericksburg refugees were rolling in, "heaps" of them.

The day became a chaos of men without arms or legs, and barking medical personnel. Though there was the rare instinctive howl of pain, Louisa heard hardly a peep from the men themselves, no matter how cruel their wounds, and at times she longed to roar and moan for them "when pride kept their white lips shut, while great drops stood upon their foreheads, and the beds shook with the irrepressible tremor of their tortured bodies."

Before the morning was out, the nurse in charge of the ward bolted from the hospital without notice, leaving inexperienced Louisa in charge of forty beds arranged in what had once been a ballroom. She toweled faces, handed around medicine, and did her best to seem capable and calm. One soldier died almost as soon as he arrived, and then she sat by another, a boy with pneumonia, draping her mother's shawl over his shoulders while he struggled for breath. He smiled faintly, murmuring, "You are real motherly, ma'am," and Louisa tried to take courage. "My thirty years made me feel old, and the suffering . . . made me long to comfort everyone."

She gripped her brown soap block "manfully," walking her basin and sponge from bed to bed to scrub away battlefield mud and cleanse putrid wounds. Louisa dabbed gently at fevered brows, delivered water (or bread, soup, meat, and coffee to those who could stomach it), and tried not to tear up over boys with stumps for arms and legs.

With ether at a premium, "the poor souls had to bear their pains as best they might," even during harrowing amputations. Louisa learned to dress wounds by assisting a surgeon who went at a "dilapidated body . . . with the enthusiasm of an accomplished seamstress."

As the day wore on, Louisa helped a right-handed man with a shattered arm write a letter to his sweetheart with the left; another, who had been shot through the stomach, pleaded for water, and by the time she returned with a cupful, he had died. There was no time to linger or reflect. Louisa kept moving, and until she turned in for the night, sometime after eleven, she cleaned and nursed and comforted her charges, even singing lullabies when the situation seemed right.

A routine soon formed, with her days beginning at six a.m. After hurriedly washing and dressing by gaslight, she braved the outrage of the men by throwing open the window in her ward to let the winter air blast through. The cold was better than the damp pestilence of an unventilated sick ward with its stew of smells: open wounds, odors drifting in from the washroom and kitchen, or from the stables outdoors. Even fresh air didn't ease the stench much, so she sprinkled lavender water while she stoked fires, adjusted blankets, and distributed breakfast—usually fried beef, salty buttered bread, and "washy" coffee. She teased and talked with her charges, or read to them from the Dickens novels she had brought with her from home. Sometimes she held the cold, clenching hands of the soldiers in their last agonized moments of life.

Louisa wrote letters home for the men, in addition to writing her own. A typical letter to May or Abby ended with "Regards to Plato," a nod to her esteemed but impractical father. The task she found most difficult was answering letters sent to soldiers who had not survived to receive them.

A young surgeon assigned to her ward, Dr. John Winslow—"Dr. John," he asked her to call him—sometimes invited her out walking. They also attended a sermon at the Capitol together and had dinner at a German restaurant (both dull, in her estimation). Dr. John quoted poetry and was "given to confidences in the twilight," but while Louisa found him "amiably amusing," he was also "exceeding young," and she kept her distance.

She volunteered for the night shift, in part so she could take her customary long morning runs. (Her route brought her to a steep hill, from which she could watch the army wagons carrying replacement troops and supplies, and see distant tufts of smoke from cannon fire.) Louisa shared a ward with "a black-eyed widow" who relieved her at dawn.

"It was a strange life—asleep half the day, exploring Washington the other half, and all night hovering, like a massive cherubim . . . over the slumbering souls of man. . . . I liked it, and found many things to amuse, instruct, and interest me. The snores alone were quite a study." After a week of listening to the "band of wind instruments" on her ward, she began to distinguish and recognize the men by their snoring.

Louisa found that watching over the men while they slept—she called her vigil "owling"—gave her an intimate glimpse into their inner worlds. "Some grow stern and grim," she wrote, "evidently dreaming of war as they give orders, groan over their wounds, or damn the rebels vigorously. Some grow infinitely sad, as if the pain bore silently all day revenges itself by now betraying what . . . pride had concealed so well. One drummer boy sang sweetly though no persuasions could win a note from him by day."

For several nights, Louisa observed a Virginia blacksmith named John Suhre while he slept. Twenty-eight years old and unmarried when the war began, Suhre had remained loyal to the

Union when his state had seceded. Fredericksburg had been his first battle and would be his last.

While awake, Suhre seemed so strong and so dignified in his bearing that Louisa gave him a wide berth. "A most attractive face he had," she wrote, "thoughtful and often beautifully mild while watching the afflictions of others as if forgetful of his own." His eyes were like a child's, she observed, "with a clear straightforward gaze," and he seemed to have "learned the secret of content."

It shocked her to learn that of all the cases in the ward, John Suhre's was the most grave. A bullet had entered his left lung and cracked a rib. Every single breath poked him like a blade. He would not recover.

When the attending surgeon asked Louisa to inform Suhre that his case was terminal, she took on the terrible task. He bore the news with his usual stoicism, but later Louisa saw him tear up in silence. "Straightaway my fear vanished," she wrote, "my heart opened wide and took him in, as, gathering the big head in my arms as freely as if he had been a little child, I said, 'Let me help you bear it, John.' Never on any human countenance have I seen so swift and beautiful a look of gratitude, surprise, and comfort. 'Thank you ma'am, this is right good! This is what I wanted.'"

It was a powerful moment for Louisa, one that locked in

all she already knew or sensed about human relations: that the best—and truest—thing we can do with our lives is share the burden of adversity.

From there, whenever his wounds were dressed, she took his hand and let him squeeze hers hard to relieve his pain. She eased him back against the pillows and gently smoothed the hair from his face.

John died two days later, a model of quiet fortitude, and she laid a sprig of heath and heliotrope on his pillow and helped prepare his body for burial. At some point, the ward matron handed Louisa a letter that had been overlooked the night before. "It was John's," Louisa wrote, and had arrived "just an hour too late to gladden the eyes that had longed and looked for it so eagerly; yet he had it." Louisa "kissed this good son for [his mother's] sake, and laid the letter in his hand." She slid off the wedding ring John's widowed mother had given him to wear in battle, clipped a lock of his hair, and sent both back to Virginia.

Louisa saw more than her share of death during her six weeks in Washington, and these very real experiences may have helped her look head-on at the loss of her beloved mentor, Thoreau.

One night as she sat by a dying soldier, she reached for a sheet of paper, and by the end of her shift, she had scribbled down a poem, "Thoreau's Flute," which opens:

We, sighing, said, "Our Pan is dead;
His pipe hangs mute beside the river;—
Around his wistful sunbeams quiver,
But Music's airy voice is fled.
Spring mourns as for untimely frost;
The bluebird chants a requiem;
The willow-blossom waits for him;—
The Genius of the wood is lost."

The poem then takes a comforting turn:

Then from the flute, untouched by hands,
There came a low, harmonious breath:
"For such as he there is no death."

Louisa filed the poem away and wouldn't look at it again for months.

Gazing out the window of her ward at night, at a church spire framed in moonlight or a boat drifting along the Potomac, Louisa understood that no river could cleanse the bloodstains from the land. But her own innocent ideas about the glory and thrill of battle had been rinsed away. Nursing changed and matured Louisa, who had learned most of what she knew about life from books and idealistic parents. For the first time, she was seeing life unfiltered—vivid and raw, teeming with real stories and real suffering.

On New Year's Eve, at midnight, Louisa's spirits soared for the first time in a long while when the church bells began to ring, signaling that the Emancipation Proclamation that President Lincoln had signed the previous September had officially gone into effect, liberating enslaved people in rebel states. Every captive in the US was now, at least on paper, free. Louisa "danced" from her bed and, to her roommate's chagrin, threw open the window, cheering and waving to a group of African American men celebrating down in the streets. All that night, Georgetown rang with tooting horns, firecrackers, and rounds of "Glory Hallelujah."

"I never began the year in a stranger place than this," she wrote on the first day of 1863, "five hundred miles from home among strangers, doing painful duties all day long and leading a life of constant excitement in this great house surrounded by 3 or 4 hundred men in all stages of suffering, disease and death. Though often homesick heartsick and worn out, I like it."

Louisa claimed that before she became a nurse, she was never sick a day in her life—a slight exaggeration, though she was healthy, hardy, and athletic—but she wasn't long at the hospital before she developed a nagging cough.

In a climate of overwork and poor diet, surrounded by disease, Civil War nurses were uniquely vulnerable, and those nurses who "in their sympathy forget that they are mortal," as she put it, were more vulnerable still. Despite her weakened state a few weeks into her assignment, Louisa never let up in her duties and continued to run every morning. Colleagues cautioned her not to wear herself down. Louisa ignored them.

A reeling headache forced her to retreat upstairs one day. "Ordered to keep [to] my room being threatened with pneumonia. Sharp pain in the side, cough, fever & dizziness. A pleasant prospect for a lonely soul five hundred miles from home!" She staggered upstairs and for days couldn't get out of bed or make it down for meals. Her fellow nurses and doctors rallied around her, and kind Dr. Winslow now knocked on her door not with social invitations or books to loan but as a worried doctor.

"I was learning that one of the best methods of fitting oneself to be a nurse in a hospital," Louisa wrote home, "is to be a patient there; for then only can one wholly realize what the men suffer and sigh for; how acts of kindness touch and win; how much or little we are to those about us."

Her recent letters had filled Bronson with foreboding. "This will end in her breaking down presently," he predicted, and he was right. When the flow of letters stopped, Orchard House simmered with unease.

Her cough grew ragged and constant. Her body didn't seem to belong to her, and her mind clouded with fever. The staff made a diagnosis: typhoid pneumonia. Louisa, who hated to appear weak, kept up a brave front and tried to take on sewing projects for the men, but she grew worse and worse. "Hours began to get confused; people looked odd; queer faces haunted the room, and the nights were one long fight with weariness and pain."

The hospital matron too had been confined to bed, gravely ill. "Dream awfully," Louisa wrote, "and awake unrefreshed, think of home and wonder if I am to die here as Mrs. Ropes is likely to do."

On the morning of January 14, the Alcotts received a telegram from Mrs. Ropes, notifying the family that both she and Louisa were bedridden. The matron's own case was dire, and Mrs. Ropes urged someone to come for Louisa at once.

Bronson caught the noon train and retraced the journey his daughter had made just weeks earlier. Standing on the threshold of Louisa's cold room in Georgetown, he counted five windowpanes broken. (No one, under the circumstances, had had time to replace them.) He heard rats in the walls. The only objects in the room beyond what Louisa had come in with were a cloudy mirror, a blue pitcher, a tin basin, and a pair of yellow mugs.

Looking up from a stark iron bed, Louisa recognized the "grey-headed gentleman [who] rose like a ghost" above her, but Bronson scarcely recognized her. His daughter looked bleached and wasted, and he choked back emotion, eager to bring her home at once, though her doctors objected. She wasn't strong enough. "Was amazed to see father enter my room that morning," Louisa wrote later, "by order of Mrs. Ropes without asking [my] leave. I was very angry at first, though glad to see him, because I knew I should have to go."

Agitated but banned from his Louisa's bedside, Bronson looked in on her patients. He was quickly relieved, as Louisa had been, of romantic notions about glory on the battlefield. "Horrid war," he wrote in his journal, "one sees its horrors in hospitals."

On January 20, Mrs. Ropes died, and the next day, Louisa was released, though heavy rains pushed their journey out a day. Dorothea Dix herself appeared at the train station to see the dedicated nurse off and to help make her comfortable.

All she later remembered of her father's presence by her sickbed was his hoarse plea: "Come home."

"At the sight of him," she wrote later, "my resolution melted away, [and] my heart turned traitor to my boys. . . . I answered 'Yes, father.'"

FRANK LESLIE'S
POPULAR MONTHLY.

Vol. XVII.— No. 3.　　　　　MARCH, 1884.　　　　　$2.50 Per Annum.

≥14≤

MERCENARY
CREATURE

1863-1865

Taking the hint I went where glory awaited me.

—Louisa May Alcott, journal, June 1863

*B*ronson and Louisa traveled all day and into the night, reached Boston in late January, and stayed overnight with Abby's relatives. When they arrived in Concord the next day, Louisa saw her condition mirrored in "May's shocked face at the Depot." By the time they entered Orchard House, Louisa was delirious, and her mother's "bewildered" expression echoed May's.

Louisa crawled into bed "in the firm belief that the house was roofless & no one wanted to see me." Her family could only try to follow her logic as her fever spiked and her hallucinations so absorbed her that she took pains to write them down. The most "vivid and enduring" delusion was that she had somehow "married a stout handsome Spaniard dressed in black velvet with very soft hands who kept saying, 'lie still, my dear.' This was Mother," she speculated later, "always coming after me, appearing out of closets."

In her confusion, Louisa pleaded for forgiveness—much as she had as a child, one who'd tried and failed, time and again, to be good. In some hallucinations she was a source of evil; in others, she was persecuted. She imagined "a mob at Baltimore breaking down the door to get me, being hung for a witch, burned, stoned," and otherwise punished. In still another vision, she arrived at a "very busy and dismal and ordinary" heaven, only to wish she hadn't.

One hallucination was so powerful, she flung herself out of bed and onto the floor. She believed that she was nursing at the Union Hotel Hospital again, "tending to millions of sick men who never died or got well."

Louisa tossed and turned for at least two days—lost between sleep and bizarre dreams, only half-aware of her anxious audience—and she didn't fully emerge for weeks. She "enjoyed" her delusions—what she remembered of them, that is, or what her family related later—"very much, at least the crazy part." The odd story lines that fascinated Louisa in retrospect must have terrified her family, stationed at her bedside during the ordeal, with occasional help from Sophia Hawthorne; Emerson's wife, Lidian; and other friends. The illness and the experiences preceding it had changed her neighbor so much, Sophia Hawthorne said, that she wouldn't have been able to pick out Louisa on the street.

Anna was seven months pregnant by then and eighteen miles away in Chelsea, but Bronson wrote her every day with his customary optimism. Behind doors, Louisa's parents were sorry they'd let their daughter go to war. "Poor Louy left us a brave handsome woman . . . and returned almost a wreck of mind and body," Abby wrote her brother Sam. Had they known the real risks, Bronson told his mother, "their contribution to the war . . . should not have been made willingly."

Next-door neighbor Julian Hawthorne, visiting two weeks after Louisa's homecoming, could hardly equate the "hollow-eyed, almost fleshless wreck" with "the Louisa we had known and loved." The worst of the sickness was past, but it was still impossible to believe that a couple of months earlier, he had delivered "a big, lovable, tender-hearted, generous girl with . . . flashing eyes" to Boston to begin her journey south. His friend was now a "white tragic mask of what she had been."

Though Louisa's spirit was slowly seeping back, "there were occasional tones in her voice and expressions that indicated depths of which she could not speak."

While snow tumbled outside the window, Bronson sat with his daughter long into the nights, talking or reading aloud, and before long she was talking back.

Louisa was often driven to frustrated tears because her legs "wouldn't go," and when she looked into the mirror, "a queer, thin big-eyed face" with shorn hair looked back. Before it had been cut by doctor's orders, her rich chestnut mane had dangled almost to the floor when loose from its pins. Her hair had been her "one beauty," Louisa believed, and she mourned the loss of it (while acknowledging wryly, "it might have been my head").

With his Louy on the mend, Bronson resumed his meetings for conversations. He was "tired out with taking care of me," Louisa joked, "poor old gentleman. . . . Typhus was not inspiring."

Abby nursed Louisa tirelessly, though, and by March, Louisa was able to sit up in bed, feed herself, and sort through papers. When she was at last strong enough to leave her room for the first time, it was to join May and Abby at the parlor window, where all three waited breathlessly as Bronson tramped toward them through the snow. Beaming, he ducked in from the storm—"all wet and white"—and waved his bag in the air like a flag. "Anna's boy," he announced, "yes, yes. Anna's boy."

"Mother began to cry, May to laugh, and I to say, 'There, I knew it wouldn't be a girl.'"

Louisa couldn't yet travel to visit Anna and John's new baby, Frederick ("Freddy"), but sent love in a note signed, "Ever your admiring Rack a bones Lu."

The ordeal at the hospital had taken a serious toll: Louisa would never fully recover her health, and memories of what she had witnessed scarred her. Moody to begin with, she now carried an air of gravity and melancholy.

But when she could manage to get out and around, Louisa ambled down Lexington Road in her granny cap, and the world seemed "beautiful and new."

"To go very near to death teaches one the value of life and this winter will always be a very memorable one to me," she wrote.

Her nursing experience would also change her as a writer. Louisa now felt that she had real stories to tell, and writing was soon at the front of her thoughts again. She was no longer a young upstart, peddling her wares along Boston's Publishers' Row, but a professional author and her family's breadwinner.

Frank Sanborn and his co-editor at the anti-slavery weekly *Commonwealth* had asked to make a series out of her letters sent home from the hospital. Her observations were "witty and sympathetic," they thought. Louisa needed income, and so she agreed, changing only minor details and fictionalizing the names. (Nurse Louisa became the very Dickensian "Tribulation Periwinkle.")

The *Commonwealth* published part one in May 1863, and readers eager for intimate knowledge of the war clamored for more. All of New England waited for the second weekly installment, a moving account of the death of John Suhre.

"I find," she wrote, "I've done a good thing without knowing it."

Two publishers approached her with offers to release her letters in book form, and she accepted the better offer. The letters were published together in a volume called *Hospital Sketches,* which became her first bestseller. The *Boston Evening Transcript* praised Louisa's "quiet humor and lively wit" and the "singular power and effectiveness" of her account. The *Roxbury Journal* pronounced her "one of the raciest and most delightful of our young female authors" and called the sketches "a new variety of literature . . . fresh and deeply interesting."

The popularity of *Hospital Sketches* baffled Louisa. "I can't see why people like a few extracts from topsy-turvy letters written on inverted tea kettles, waiting for gruel to warm or poultices to cool."

But she came to understand that her realism and candor had reached people. Later, she would credit the book with pointing her in the right literary direction. "*Sketches* never made much money, but showed me '*my style,*' & taking the hint I went where glory awaited me."

Bronson and Abby, meanwhile, had found "Thoreau's Flute" among Louisa's things and read it to "neighbor Hawthorne." Sophia sent it to Annie Fields, who shared it with her husband. When the *Atlantic* published "Thoreau's Flute" that September (anonymously, per custom), America's most famous poet, Henry

Wadsworth Longfellow, praised it, speculating that Emerson was the author. Not so, Bronson was quick to point out.

"Had a fresh feather in my cap," Louisa boasted, "for Mrs. Hawthorne showed Fields 'Thoreau's Flute' & he desired it for the Atlantic. Of course I didn't say No. It was printed, copied praised & glorified—also *paid* for, & being a mercenary creature I liked the $10 nearly as well as the honor."

The mercenary creature continued to live a double life as an author, sending her sensational blood-and-thunder tales to the weeklies, which published them anonymously or under an assumed name. When "Pauline's Passion and Punishment" (the story Louisa had secretly submitted to the contest in Frank Leslie's newspaper before she'd left for Washington) won the hundred-dollar first prize, she paid off some Alcott debts and spent the rest on a set of furniture for her room—a dresser and a big mahogany sleigh bed. Since she wouldn't require furniture if she boarded in Boston, the purchase seemed to mark a decision to stay on at Orchard House. Was she too exhausted to resume her independent life, or just grateful for home?

* * *

Louisa lived in Concord for the duration of the war, writing at top speed to meet the sudden demand for her work. The success of *Hospital Sketches* and her secret commercial hit with "Pauline's Passion and Punishment" had put her on the map, stabilizing her career as a professional author after long years spent laboring as a seamstress, servant, and teacher in addition to writing.

"Pauline's Passion and Punishment" was only the first of many tales accepted by publishing titan Frank Leslie, who soon commissioned one racy thriller each month at fifty dollars per story, five times what she'd earned for a poem in the prestigious *Atlantic*. "I can't afford to starve on praise," she wrote, "when sensation stories are written in half the time and keep the family cosey."

In the careful memorandum of earnings that Louisa kept throughout her writing career, it's clear that blood-and-thunder tales published by Leslie and by a weekly called the *Flag of Our Union*, with titles such as "A Whisper in the Dark" and "A Pair of Eyes," were the high earners by a long shot.

What Louisa called her "rubbishy" tales would fund the Alcott family for years to come, and her editors agreed that if listing her name on her sensational stories would hurt her career as a children's book author, "Mr. Leslie would not desire any such sacrifice."

"All my dreams are getting fulfilled in the most amazing way," Louisa wrote in her journal in October 1863. "A year ago I had no publisher and went begging with my wares, now three have asked me for something. There is a sudden hoist for a meek and lowly scribbler who was told to 'stick to her teaching.'"

Back in January, she had nearly been a casualty of the Civil War. A few short months later, Louisa found herself one of the most celebrated women in New England.

Riding that success, she applied as a volunteer to travel to Port Royal, South Carolina, to teach contrabands—people who had escaped from slavery into the protection of the Union army.

James Fields of the *Atlantic* heard of Louisa's plans and offered to publish her letters home if she went. (The bestselling *Hospital Sketches* must have further persuaded the once-skeptical editor that Louisa could write, after all.) Her Port Royal application was turned down because she didn't have a male chaperone to accompany her to South Carolina, but Fields accepted a relevant story instead, a tragic tale called "My Contraband," about brothers on opposite sides of the slavery debate.

* * *

Louisa continued to aid the war effort in other ways also. She and May sewed sleeping bags and uniforms for soldiers. The sisters advocated for universal access to literacy—still legally denied to former slaves—and donated books to classes at the Readville barracks of the United States Colored Troops (USCT), for Union regiments of African American and other minority soldiers. Louisa traveled to Boston to cheer them on as they marched toward South Carolina. (The clashes at Fort Wagner ended in a sound Union defeat, but with the first US African American regiment fighting, the clashes were also bold strokes for freedom.)

Louisa was moved to take out her nursing uniform that fall when a company of sixty young Concord soldiers, veterans of Gettysburg, came home to flags flying. The town drum corps, eight small boys wrestling eight big drums, thumped out a march while Julian Hawthorne made enough lemonade "to flavor Walden Pond." May and other "fair ladies" of Concord passed around refreshments.

The proud hospital veteran had no idea that the company planned to march past Orchard House, where the captain called a halt and the young men pivoted and raised their caps to salute the famous author and army nurse, before dropping back into ranks and marching on.

* * *

Also that fall, at the request of a well-connected friend, Louisa fished her pet project, the serious literary novel *Moods*, out of its spidery cabinet, breaking her vow never to look at it again. "I let her have it," Louisa wrote, "hoping she might be able to give the poor old book the lift it has [been] waiting for all these three years. She took it, read it & admired it heartily."

The friend sent the manuscript to publisher A. K. Loring, who suggested—as others had before him—that Louisa shorten it. If she did, he would like to publish it.

Louisa awoke one night soon after with a revision plan. She never got back to sleep "but worked on it busily as if mind & body had nothing to do with one another." This time her vortex lasted two weeks, and she excised ten chapters. Loring praised the story "more enthusiastically than ever, thanking me for the improvements, & proposing to bring out the book at once. Of course we all had a rapture."

But when Loring sent page proofs of *Moods* for Louisa to review, the novel seemed to her "small, stupid & no more my own." What had begun as an ambitious psychological study of her heroine, Sylvia Yule, had become—with editing, nipping, and tucking—a convoluted romance.

Even so, the first edition sold out in days.

She received her publication copy on Christmas 1864, in time to gift it to her mother and thank Abby for her sympathy, love, and help over many years of challenge and hardship. "I hope success will sweeten me and make me what I long to become more than a great writer—a good daughter."

Abby read the book almost cover to cover that Christmas night before bed. Bronson would read it just as eagerly.

"For a week wherever I went I saw, heard, & talked 'moods;' found people laughing or crying over it. . . . I was glad but not proud, I think." Overall, public response was mixed. The soon-to-be-famous novelist Henry James Jr., son of a friend of Bronson's, wrote a harsh, dismissive review: "The two most striking facts with regard to *Moods* are the author's ignorance of human nature, and her self-confidence in spite of this ignorance." Damning with faint praise, he noted, "With the exception of two or three celebrated names, we know not, indeed, to whom, in the country, unless to Miss Alcott, we are to look for a novel above the average."

In other words, Louisa had not lived up to her promise, and in private, she agreed. "*Moods* is not what I meant."

Despite her reservations, the novel went into a third printing.

On and off, Louisa would circle back to her other serious project, *Success*. (The title changed to *Work* before publication.) But for now her serialized thrillers—some published under the name A. M. Barnard—were selling at a brisk clip.

She would fall "back on rubbishy tales" for a while, she told Alf Whitman. They were less work, more fun, and more lucrative.

The *Flag of Our Union* serialized *V.V.: or, Plots and Counterplots,* a short novel of "several hundred pages" that Louisa had dashed off "to relieve [her] feelings" while *Moods* incubated in its spidery cupboard. Other publishers were clamoring for new work too, and offering competitive pay. "Alcott brains seem in demand," the author noted with pride.

While Louisa worked away at her little crescent-shaped desk at Orchard House that spring, the Civil War was simmering to its close.

Union general William Tecumseh Sherman had captured Savannah, Georgia, the previous December, and on April 9, 1865, General Robert E. Lee surrendered the Confederate Army of Northern Virginia to the Union's Ulysses S. Grant at Appomattox Court House, Virginia.

Two weeks after Louisa had attended the great Shakespearean actor Edwin Booth's Boston performance as Hamlet, rating it "finer than ever," Booth's brother, John Wilkes Booth, assassinated President Lincoln on April 14, 1865.

In the North, "grand jollification" over the end of the war

was eclipsed that April by grief. Bronson and many others appreciated Lincoln more profoundly after Booth fired his bullet. When word reached Concord of the tragedy that took place at Ford's Theatre, the slain president was elevated, almost overnight, to the status of "martyr" and "cherished idol."

Passionate abolitionists led a solemn procession in Boston, and Louisa took quiet pride in her own sacrifices in support of freedom and equality.

The Alcotts felt a similar mix of joy and sadness when Anna gave birth to a second son on June 24, what would have been Lizzie's thirtieth birthday.

Named after his father, the baby was delivered by Alcott cousin Lucy Sewall—among the first women in America to earn a medical degree and launch a practice. Louisa judged her new nephew "a fine little lad who took to life kindly & seemed to find the world all right."

While she was helping Anna and John with the new addition, Louisa received a tempting invitation.

"Mr Wm F. Weld hearing that I was something of a nurse & wanted to travel proposed my going with his invalid daughter," Louisa wrote in her journal. The rich Boston merchant hoped Louisa might play companion to his daughter Anna, escorted by his son George, in Europe for a year.

Louisa didn't know the Welds and hesitated—perhaps

recalling her disastrous job in Dedham with predatory Mr. Richardson—but her family and friends urged her to seize what might be the opportunity of a lifetime. To Louisa, it was a chance to fulfill a "long-desired dream."

It took her a week to decide, pack, and organize.

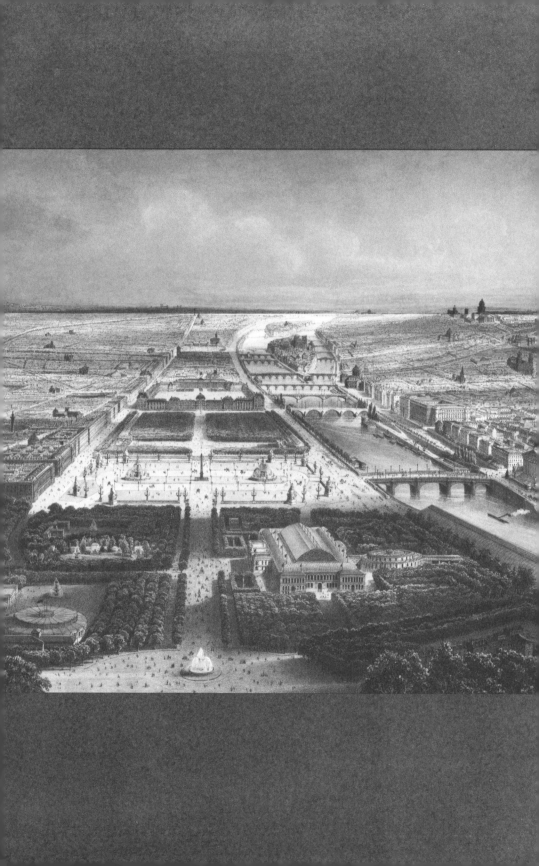

➤15➤

MI
DROGHA

1865-1866

We led a happy life together.

—Louisa May Alcott, "Aunt Jo's Scrap Bag

*I*t was only when the Cunard steamship *China* chuffed out of Boston Harbor on July 20, 1865, that reality dawned: a whole year away. "I might not see all the dear home faces, when I come back," Louisa fretted.

Three years younger than Louisa, twenty-nine-year-old Anna Weld was the spoiled baby of her father's first marriage. Anna's twenty-five-year-old half brother, George, was a fashionable young man around town. It was immediately obvious that he and Louisa had nothing in common, and the trip over was worse than jarring. Louisa spent most of it in the "Ladies Saloon," probably more seasick than she let on, though she enjoyed "intervals of quiet & had many fine glimpses of the sea in its various moods. Sunsets & sun rises, fogs, icebergs, rain storms & summer calms." Anna wasn't exactly an invalid, but she was delicate, often unwell, and dull, with no interest whatsoever in literature. With "no pleasant people on board," Louisa wrote, "I read & whiled away the long days as best I could."

The disingenuous nature of their arrangement riled Louisa. On the one hand, she was being paid—to travel the world with an inoffensive young person more or less her own age. On the other hand, she was being paid—and had to smile and nod at boring chatter and treat Anna's every minor whim and whine with care and attention. Louisa had to ease Anna's days by reading aloud, singing, or gingerly massaging her companion's temples with cool water while the invalid never seemed to value any of it (or get better). Louisa did her best to stay cheerful, sinking into her books and writing, and wringing pleasure from the kaleidoscopic landscape.

The *China* docked in Liverpool nine days later, much to Louisa's relief, and after a two-night layover in what Louisa deemed a dirty city teeming with beggars, they boarded a train for London and had "four dull, drizzly days." Anna was ill, and George off sightseeing, Louisa wrote, so "I amused myself in my usual way, looking well about me & writing descriptions of all I saw in letters or my pocket diary." She sheltered from the weather in dark Westminster Abbey and prowled "the famous streets" with the sense that she had "got into a novel."

In mid-August, after itinerary stops in Ostend and Brussels in Belgium, and Cologne in Germany, they boarded a boat up the Rhine full of quirky characters that gave Louisa a chance to flex her comic muscles. The English tourists "sat bolt upright as if they had made up their minds to be surprised at nothing." The French had a *bonjour* for "every mortal who approached." Americans "stared and asked questions." Many of these fellow voyagers were, like Louisa's party, bound for Schwalbach, Germany, a popular resort town and spa in the mountains near

Wiesbaden. There Anna would consult with the world-famous doctor Adolph Genth, a proponent of the water cure, a system of hydrotherapy used to treat all manner of medical ills of the day.

The party came to a "narrow valley shut in between high hills," and George delivered Anna and Louisa to their lodgings with Madame Genth, in a neighborhood near the springs "full of fine hotels, pleasant grounds & bath houses." George went off exploring, and Anna began her water treatments under Dr. Genth's care. "I tried my best to suit & serve her," Louisa wrote, "but hers is a hard case to manage & needs the patience and wisdom of an angel."

Louisa was no angel but soldiered on, helping Anna dribble down her restorative water and coaxing her out for the odd walk or ride.

When a letter from home finally caught up with Louisa in September, she relished the fact that she was not forgotten. "My absence seems to have left so large a gap that I begin to realize how much I am to them in spite of all my faults."

On September 28, George returned from his rambles to escort them to Switzerland. En route, they crossed through Frankfurt, the birthplace of an Alcott (and transcendental) idol. When Louisa begged to look in at the home of the great German author, the Welds outvoted her. "Who was Goethe to fuss about?" Anna asked.

Louisa could only flinch.

They stopped over at a "most romantic" grand hotel built over a beautiful valley. ("If only," Louisa wrote, she'd "had good company to share it with.") They then arrived in bustling Vevey, with the "white Alps of Savoy" in the background, "shining in the sun like some celestial country seen in dreams."

Eager to enjoy a few weeks in Paris, George dropped his charges off with the matron of the Pension Victoria, an English-woman.

Tucked away behind five tall poplar trees on the shore of Lake Geneva, the small hotel had lodgers "from all quarters of the world." The resort hosted a come-and-go society that in good weather strolled out onto the stone terraces, with the lake water lapping below, the air laced with the smell of fresh herbs from the kitchen garden, flowers in the window boxes, and roses on the slope behind the building.

Guests sipped tea or wine on café balconies and mingled in the salon. Among them were a Russian baron, an "overfed" Frenchman who struck Napoleonic poses, and an Irish matron swaddled in crepe who wouldn't remove her black mourning gloves even at dinner. There was the English colonel who re-lentlessly lectured his six pale little daughters on history, math-ematics, and astronomy during meals.

Louisa pitied the children, but it was another colonel—a former US Confederate named Polk—who most riled Louisa, with his rants about Yankee treachery, and his insistence that his slaves had been unhappily abducted by Northern armies and wished only to come home. For Louisa, the war might have been over, but an enemy was still easy to spot. "Col Polk & family, rebels, & very bitter & rude to us," she wrote in her journal.

Just as the novelty of the Pension Victoria was beginning to wear off—"for I missed my freedom & grew very tired"—Louisa's attentions turned to a more agreeable visitor.

One crisp autumn day in November 1865, while she warmed herself by the stove at breakfast, a stranger walked in, "a tall youth, of eighteen or twenty, with a thin, intelligent face, and the charmingly polite manners of a foreigner." As other boarders arrived and went, and the door opened and closed, cold air blew in from the stone corridor, "making the new-comer cough, shiver, and cast wistful glances towards the warm corner by the stove."

Louisa offered her spot, inching over to make room for him—"The heat often oppressed me, so I was glad"—and at dinner "was rewarded by a grateful smile from the poor fellow." They were seated too far apart to speak naturally, but as he filled his wineglass, the young man nodded and murmured in French, "I drink the good health to Mademoiselle."

She "returned the wish, but he shook his head with a sudden shadow on his face, as if the words meant more than mere compliment to him."

Louisa glimpsed him again later, passing through the salon in what appeared to be military garb. (She confessed a "weakness for brave boys in blue," though his uniform was blue and white.) The young man looked ill, perhaps tubercular, in need of a nurse. Fresh on the heels of her experiences in Washington, Louisa "warmed to him at once."

"That evening he came to me in the salon," Louisa wrote, "and in half an hour we were friends."

His name, she learned, was "Ladislas Wisniewski—two hiccoughs and a sneeze will give you the name perfectly."

She also learned that Ladislas—Louisa called him "Laddie"—had taken part, with other students, in the recent Polish rebellion. He had been jailed for his role in the uprising and had contracted tuberculosis (TB) in prison, losing "many friends, his fortune and his health."

Laddie described a massacre in which "five hundred Poles were shot down by Cossacks in the market-place, merely because they sung their national hymn." (Louisa heard him practicing piano "softly" that afternoon and urged, "Play me that forbidden air.")

Not only did Laddie speak to Louisa's ideas of heroism— "in the prettiest broken English I ever heard"—but he was also vulnerable and poetic, a musician, and young enough for her to nurse or mother while keeping her romantic distance. He even called her "little mamma" during their time together, though his flirting suggested that his feelings were more complicated. He also told her that the word *drogha* meant "friend" in Polish. She repeated it often, only to learn later that saying *mi drogha* was as good as saying "my darling," "in the tenderest manner."

At twenty, "lonely, poor, and ill," Laddie planned to travel to Paris and teach music, assuming he recovered.

Each evening throughout her stay, Laddie presented Louisa with a rose at the dinner table. Afterward, while the older residents played cards, Louisa and Laddie huddled in a corner of the salon, teaching each other their native languages. Laddie had four or five languages under his belt already and excelled, though he slapped his head and moaned, "I am imbecile! I never can will shall to have learn this beast of English!"

Once the torrent of words started, Louisa wrote, "the barrier of an unknown language did not long stand between us."

Years after her European tour, Louisa kept and cherished the "pile of merry little notes" that had been tucked under her door, chapters in "a great history we were to write together."

While the "little romance" with Laddie lasted, the Pension Victoria was the perfect picturesque background for it. Louisa and Laddie took long walks and made "splendid plans for the future."

Louisa learned that Laddie and another pianist staying at

the pension often performed for the guests informally, and on her birthday, he played "his sweetest airs as a present," wishing her "all good & happiness on earth."

She wrote that the "wild and windy day" was "like me in its fitful changes of sunshine & shade. Usually I am sad on my birthday but not this time. I feel rather old with my 33 years but have much to keep me younger and hope I shall not grow older in heart as the time goes on."

When Anna Weld decided to move on to warmer climes, Louisa and Laddie "jokingly agreed" to meet in Paris in May. "I felt sure I would soon be forgotten," she wrote. "As he kissed my hand, there were tears in my boy's eyes and a choke in the voice that tried to say cheerfully—'*Bon voyage,* dear and good little mamma. I do not say *adieu,* but *au revoir.*'"

Until we meet again.

Laddie followed Louisa and the Welds as far as Lausanne, and when the US group set out for Nice on the French Riviera, he turned back, "disconsolate."

After a few weeks in Nice, Louisa "tired of doing nothing pleasing or interesting." The city and its fashionable Promenade, where "every one was on exhibition," left her cold, and she reported "a dull Christmas within doors." Outside, the roses were in full bloom. The air was sweet and mild. Nice seemed a happy, bustling place, with perpetual summer; but without money, true friendship, and robust health, Louisa was in no mind to enjoy it.

Anna rarely left her bed, and though Louisa could sometimes slip out for a walk through the vineyards and olive groves, she felt suffocated and trapped.

By February 1866, she was fed up altogether and made a difficult choice: she would head home to Concord in May. "Tired of it," she wrote, "and as Anna is not going to travel my time is too valuable to be spent fussing over cushions and carrying shawls. . . . She wears on me & we are best apart."

Though Louisa lured Anna out for a few jaunts around the countryside, their last weeks were tedious, Louisa wrote, when the time "might have been quite the reverse had I been able to enjoy it in my own way." Their friendship for hire was fraying at the edges, and once she'd decided to leave, Louisa found it difficult to keep up a front. She couldn't sleep and "felt very poorly for my life didn't suit me & the air was too exciting."

Stunned and worried that their Lu would rather come home than explore Europe with the Welds, Bronson urged her to drain every drop from her time abroad. He had four hundred dollars, he wrote, from his tour in the West, and Louisa's uncle Sam May would see them another hundred. Louisa deserved to stay on and enjoy her opportunities overseas.

Louisa took him up on it.

In May, she left Anna in the care of George and a new companion and lit out by train for her liberty in Paris, where she would spend two weeks at Madame Dyne's pension.

She would never again take employment that didn't involve her pen.

And there was someone waiting for her at the station.

After they got Louisa settled in her pension, Laddie led a whirlwind of sightseeing in the enchanted city.

Louisa had her first glimpse of the Louvre. They lingered over romantic café lunches and shopped—with Laddie managing the negotiations "in the best of French."

There were "quiet strolls in the gardens, moonlight concerts in the Champs Elysées," and "best of all, long talks with music in the little red salon, with the gas turned low, and the ever-changing scenes of the Rue de Rivoli under the balcony."

They avoided the heat and crowds of the theater or balls in favor of "pleasant trips out of the city in the bright spring weather."

Louisa wrote that day after day "I fearlessly went anywhere on the arm of my big son."

* * *

She kissed him tenderly when they said goodbye, then "ran away and buried myself in an empty railway carriage, hugging the little cologne bottle he had given me."

Did Bronson and Abby know about those weeks, which Louisa admitted were "the pleasantest fortnight in all my year of travel"? Her journals and letters give few clues, but it was highly unusual at the time—and terrifically bold—for a respectable single lady to liaise with a man in a foreign city for days and weeks without a chaperone. "My twelve years' seniority made our adventures quite proper," she wrote, and despite Laddie's romantic nature and gestures, they both seemed to view the time as sweet but fleeting.

For Louisa, who boarded her train out of Paris "feeling as if in this world there were no more meetings for us," Laddie was her last and possibly only real love interest.

In her journal, she scratched out passages of an entry beginning, "A little romance with Laddie," and later added, "couldn't be."

Louisa had sixteen days with Laddie in Paris, enough to say later, "We led a happy life together."

AUGUST,
1868.

MERRY'S MUSEUM,

An Illustrated Magazine for Boys and Girls.

Vol. 1.   No. 8

NEW SERIES.

BOSTON: H. B. FULLER.

PRICE . . . . 15 . . . . CENTS.

➤*16*➤

NEVER
LIKED
GIRLS

1866-1868

Wonder if I shall ever be famous enough for people
to care to read my story and struggles. . . .
I may do a little something yet.

—Louisa May Alcott, journal, June 1857

*I*f Louisa missed Laddie, no one knew. She next spent seven weeks in London. For the rest of May and June, she drew on her high connections. Louisa ate, drank, and rubbed elbows with the city's literary elite and attended concerts and lectures. She even got to hear one of her heroes read, though she was disappointed to discover that Charles Dickens, with his "foppish curls . . . false teeth and the voice of a worn-out actor," was a literary celebrity past his prime.

In early July, she came full circle in Liverpool, where she boarded the steamship *Africa* for home. Seasick and bored, Louisa worried the whole way, about her parents—particularly Abby's health—and the state of the family's finances.

While Louisa had still been in Europe, Bronson had written to her to say how excited they all were to see her and, as if anticipating her worry and the duties to come, had urged, "Get all you can before setting your face homewards." He was proud of her—his "noble daughter"—and said so. "The doors are opened wide for the freest exercise of your good Gifts, fame, if you must have it, and a world wide influence."

When Louisa arrived at Orchard House, May flew "wildly around the lawn" while their mother lingered in the doorway, tears streaming. Abby looked older—sick and tired—and it struck Louisa how bravely her mother had endured, how much she had sacrificed. "I never expected to see the strong, energetic 'marmee' of old times, but thank the Lord she is still here."

Abby was sixty-five, elderly by the standards of the day, and when Louisa let herself go limp in her mother's arms, she knew that she was home. As aware as ever of her childhood promise to bring peace and rest to the woman who had sheltered the Alcotts with tireless love and strength, Louisa saw that it was Abby's time to rest and be cared for, and this powered her ambition.

Her father seemed as serene as always; May was bursting with plans; Anna was harried from chasing her two little boys around (but the boys were a pleasure). Concord was still sleepy, but for a time, Orchard House filled with friends and neighbors eager for word of her adventures.

Louisa's travels had changed her, they said, and they were right, though she didn't get to bask in her homecoming long. Louisa was soon back at her desk, filling the demand for her work and rebuilding the Alcott Sinking Fund. The family had fallen behind on bills in her absence—no surprise—and the five hundred dollars that had paid for her time in Paris and London had apparently been a figment of Bronson's well-meaning imagination.

Louisa "dread[ed] debt more than the devil," and within the week was cranking out two stories for Frank Leslie at one hundred dollars each, a novella for James Elliot of the *Flag of Our Union,* and a short novel called *Behind a Mask; or, a Woman's Power,* a sharp twist on Charlotte Brontë's *Jane Eyre* (and a spin on her own unpublished first novel, *The Inheritance,* written when she was seventeen).

For six months she wrote sometimes fourteen hours a day, and when Abby was unwell, Louisa hired a household servant to cook and clean so that she could care for her mother by day and write and pay bills ("never expect to see the end of em," she quipped) late into the night.

When she added up her annual earnings, Louisa discovered that they were higher than ever, yet no match for the Alcotts' skyrocketing debt. Haunted by a lifetime spent scraping by— dependent on borrowed money, food baskets, and hand-me-downs, waking up in borrowed houses—Louisa "wrote 12 tales in three months," and the stress and pressure leveled her.

Frank Sanborn wrote to a mutual friend, "Louisa Alcott has been alarmingly ill . . . her head overworked and taking revenge." Louisa's diagnosis was the same as Sanborn's: "Sick from too hard work. Did nothing all month but sit in a dark room & ache. Head and eyes full of neuralgia."

Of her adventure as a nurse, she liked to say, "I was never

ill before this time, and never well afterward," and with good reason.

In Washington, army doctors had treated typhoid fever and pneumonia with heavy, repeated doses of calomel, a so-called cure that was standard at the time, derived from mercury. Without knowing it, they had poisoned Louisa, and she would suffer sore throats, searing headaches, odd oral sensations, leg pain, and nervous exhaustion for most of the rest of her life—and sometimes be disabled for months at a time. She had always suffered severe mood swings too, and the burdens of playing tireless nurse to her mother and literary "golden goose" to the family, along with Anna's boys frolicking underfoot, were a combined assault on her inner resources. She spent that January 1867 in her dark room aching, unable to write again until late spring.

By July she was working at full tilt again, writing, performing onstage for charity, and raking in new assignments. (She wrote in her journal, "Bills accumulate and worry me.")

In the fall of that year, Louisa got two tantalizing offers; interestingly, both were in the children's market. After the war, national railroads, new printing technology, and the readiness of cheap paper had hurried the spread of mass popular culture in the United States, resulting in a new (and profitable, for publishers) demand for children's books. Louisa's first offer was an invitation from Horace Fuller to edit an illustrated children's magazine called *Merry's Museum.* The second offer was a bit more complicated.

Bronson had called on Roberts Brothers publishing about his own new project, a philosophical labor of love called *Tablets* (not the mystical manuscript that had consumed him after Fruitlands, but a graceful transcendentalist argument for living simply and mindfully in a fast-paced industrialized world). Thomas Niles, a partner in the publishing house, was enthusiastic but at the same time seized the opportunity to suggest Louisa for a project. The booming children's book market lacked good, strong, simple books for girls, and Niles thought she might be the writer to fill the void.

"Niles, partner of Roberts, asked me to write a girl's book. Said I'd try." Louisa did try, but found she had little stamina for writing children's stories other than fanciful fables like the ones she'd told Ellen Emerson. Editing *Merry's Museum* was a steady gig with an annual salary. All she had to do, in theory, was read submissions and contribute one original story and one editorial per issue, which would leave her plenty of time to churn out hundred-dollar tales for Frank Leslie and the thrillers market. She let the novel slide and used the steady income from *Merry's* to buy back her independence.

Just shy of her thirty-fifth birthday, Louisa packed up her worldly goods and heaped them into a wagon, as the Alcotts had done so many times as a family. She took her young nephew, Freddy, along for the ride, and felt she was heading off to "camp out in a new country," one she hoped would be "hospitable."

She had rented a top-floor room at 6 Hayward Place in Boston, conveniently located near Fuller's office for *Merry's Museum,* and she dubbed the room "Gamp's Garrett." Warm, safe, and free from care, Louisa gleefully resumed the independent life she had left behind years before, attending cultural events, acting for charity, eating only when she felt like it, and burning the midnight oil while the ink flowed. "I am in my little room," she wrote in early 1868, "spending busy happy days because I have quiet, freedom, work enough, and strength to do it. . . . My way seems clear for the year if I can only keep well."

In November, May took a job teaching drawing in the city and was commuting in from Concord, so Louisa's new arrangement gave her sister a comfortable place to crash when needed. Bronson too sometimes made camp at Gamp's Garrett after an evening lecture. No one seemed to begrudge Louisa the right to live away from home. She was finally accepting her own limits. Her energy had bounds, and she could do more for the Alcott cause by writing than she could by managing the day-to-day affairs of Orchard House. Her commitment to keeping the Alcott Sinking Fund plump was well established. She'd earned some thousand dollars since returning from Washington and the war.

"Keep all the money I send," she wrote to her mother, "pay up every bill, get comforts, and enjoy yourselves. Let's be merry while we may. And lay up a bit for a rainy day."

When the first potted hyacinth bloomed "white and sweet'" in her little room, she took it as a sign, a respite from "the enemies we have been fighting all these years. Perhaps we are to win after all, and conquer poverty, neglect, pain and debt and march on with flags flying."

Winter passed in a flurry of writing, editing, acting, and mingling around town. Louisa lived between literary extremes, dashing off cheery tales for *Merry's Museum* and racy fiction for Frank Leslie. "Perilous Play," one of her most risqué thrillers and one of the last blood-and-thunder tales she wrote, gave her a chance to explore romantic and sensual themes that were otherwise barred to her as an unmarried gentlewoman in her day. She had chosen single life, being prideful, and wary of marriage and its complexities. She reserved her admiration for older men such as Emerson, younger men such as Laddie and Alf Whitman, or vulnerable men such as John Suhre, who were safely inaccessible. At times, she questioned her choices, especially when she visited Anna and her family. "She is a happy woman! I sell my children," Louisa wrote, "and though they feed me, they don't love me as hers do."

But in the end, Louisa understood her own peculiar

nature—and understood that happiness takes many forms. She contributed—to an "Advice to Young Women" column in the *New York Ledger*—an argument for single life titled, "Happy Women," in which she urged young readers to choose an unconventional path, should it call to them—without fear of pity or loneliness—and to value and use their talents. "Liberty is a better husband than love to many of us."

Louisa may have given up on writing a girls' book, but her father and Thomas Niles of Roberts Brothers had other plans.

Niles hoped that the author of *Flower Fables* and editor of *Merry's Museum* would create something to rival his competitors' popular series for boys. Bronson believed that a story about the Alcott girls would surpass the moral and sentimental sludge on the market for children. He believed that real children needed to see themselves reflected in books.

Niles had agreed to publish Bronson's philosophical book but was also counting on Louisa to honor her pledge. The pressure was on. "He obviously wishes to become your publisher and mine," wrote her father. "Now . . . come home soon and write your story."

With Abby failing by degrees, Louisa gave in, and arrived in Concord ten days later.

Her mother needed her. Spring in Concord was beautiful, summer was far kinder there than in the city, and she could economize on rent.

Inspiration was hard in coming, at least at first. "I plod away," she complained, "though I don't enjoy this sort of thing. Never liked girls or knew many, except my sisters."

But in early May, Louisa dipped her quill, glancing up from the tiny half-moon desk her father had built between the windows of her room. She looked out over Lexington Road and the fields and woods of her childhood—and down again—and her pen began scratching the page.

She wrote:

"'Christmas won't be Christmas without any presents,' grumbled Jo, lying on the rug. . . ."

LITTLE WOMEN

OR,

MEG, JO, BETH AND AMY

BY LOUISA M. ALCOTT

ILLUSTRATED BY MAY ALCOTT

BOSTON
ROBERTS BROTHERS
1868

EPILOGUE

It reads better than I expected. Not a bit sensational, but simple and true, for we really lived most of it; and if it succeeds, that will be the reason.

—Louisa May Alcott, journal, August 1868

*I*n 1868, when she was thirty-five, Louisa May Alcott won the fortune and fame she had craved all her life.

Little Women was originally published in two volumes, and Louisa wrote the first half of it—all twenty-three chapters—grudgingly, in just ten weeks, without the feverish surrender she felt when writing thrillers.

At first, both she and her editor, Thomas Niles, lacked enthusiasm for her labors: "Sent twelve chapters of 'L.W.' to Mr. N. He thought it dull," she concluded. "So do I."

But Niles shared the work-in-progress with his young niece, who knew better, and Louisa vowed to keep going and "try the experiment, for lively, simple books are very much needed for girls, and perhaps I can supply the need."

When her page proofs arrived from the publisher, Louisa conceded that her four little women—the March sisters, modeled on herself (Jo), Anna (Meg), Lizzie (Beth), and May (Amy)—were the genuine article. "The characters were drawn from life," she wrote to a friend, "for I find it impossible to invent anything half so true or touching as the simple facts."

Louisa had been living in Orchard House while she'd written the book and had used that home as her setting, but *Little*

Women drew mainly on her childhood years with her sisters at Hillside.

In January 1869, she reported to her uncle Sam that volume two was "in the press & I often have letters asking when it will be out." Louisa enjoyed receiving letters from children, "for they are the best critics." But she was no fan of sequels and doubted that the new book would be as popular as its predecessor.

What's more, fans were clamoring for a wedding. It dismayed Louisa when girls wrote to ask "who the little women marry, as if that was the only end and aim of a woman's life," and she vowed, "I won't marry Jo to Laurie to please anyone." Louisa believed that, like Jo's creator, Jo should remain a "literary spinster" and "paddle [her] own canoe."

Louisa's publisher, Roberts Brothers, begged to differ.

"Publishers are very *perwerse* & won't let authors have their way," she grumped, "so my little women must grow up & be married off in a very stupid style."

If Jo was going to get married, it would be on Louisa's terms.

The character of Laurie in *Little Women* was a composite of the real-life Laddie—"the best and dearest of all" Louisa's "boys"—and Louisa's lifelong pal Alf Whitman. "All my little girl-friends are madly in love with Laurie & insist on a sequel," she reported to Whitman, "so I've written one which will make you laugh, especially the pairing off part. . . . You won't mind being a happy spouse and proud papa," she teased. "Will you?"

The mercenary creature would not disappoint her publisher but would, Louisa told Whitman, "disappoint the young gossips who vowed that Laurie and Jo should marry." Instead, she made "a funny match" for Jo in the sage but not exactly swoon-worthy Professor Bhaer, fully expecting that "vials of wrath" would be poured down on her head.

Louisa enjoyed every minute of the fight. She knew best.

Jo was *her* creation. Jo was *her*.

In modern terms, *Little Women* has been more than a publishing success. It's an international phenomenon.

Translated into more than fifty languages, the story has also been adapted "for stage, television, opera, ballet, Hollywood, Bollywood, and Japanese anime," notes biographer Harriet Reisen. The story has crossed "every cultural and religious border."

In their day, the titles in the Little Women trilogy—*Little Women, Little Men,* and *Jo's Boys*—were anticipated with "a fervor not seen again," Reisen notes, "until the Harry Potter series of J.K. Rowling."

The books have been in print ever since publication.

*   *   *

The success of the bestselling *Little Women* made Louisa a reluctant celebrity. "People begin to come and stare at the Alcotts," she wrote. "Reporters haunt the place to look at the authoress, who dodges into the woods a la Hawthorne."

Deprived of precious solitude and tired of literary "lion hunters" making unannounced pilgrimages to her home in Concord, the former actress was known to pose as her own servant to turn autograph seekers away from the door of Orchard House. "Driven to frenzy by twenty-eight visitors in a week," she even contemplated blasting uninvited visitors with water from the garden hose.

How did the wild and ungovernable child of a penniless philosopher and a brilliant but defeated mother, a tomboy who didn't "care much for girl's things," grow up to write the most famous girls' book of all time?

Call it accident, or Providence, as Bronson Alcott might have said, but the answer begins and ends with the Pathetic Family—and with sleepy Concord, Massachusetts.

As a worldly adult, Louisa complained that Concord hadn't "known a startling hue since the redcoats were there." She never felt quite at home in such a close-knit and conventional community. Louisa credited the town with hosting the happiest days of her childhood, but she also resented Concord: "I shall always be a wretched victim to [its] respectable traditions."

If she was cursed, she was also blessed.

Visiting Bronson on his deathbed in 1888, Louisa knew it would be the last time she saw him. She had always longed for her father's approval and loved him fiercely despite their rivalry and her lifelong rebellion.

"Father," she said, "here is your Louy. What are you thinking of as you lie there so happily?"

"I am going up," he rasped, pointing. "Come with me."

"Oh, I wish I could."

Bronson died a few days later, and Louisa (born on her father's thirty-third birthday) died two days after that, on March 6, 1888, at age fifty-five of a stroke.

Her body was buried on a hillside called Authors Ridge in Sleepy Hollow Cemetery in Concord, in a plot with her mother (who had died quietly in Nurse Louisa's arms eleven years earlier); father; and little sister, Lizzie; and near Ralph Waldo Emerson; Henry David Thoreau; and Nathaniel Hawthorne.

In death, as in life, the circle is unbroken.

Acknowledgments

Thanks to my agent and friend, Jill Grinberg, who always finds the perfect publishing match for a project, as if by magic, and helps shepherd each through the process with effortless grace. Thanks, too, to the whole brilliant team at Jill Grinberg Literary. You're the best.

As always, I owe a debt to creative cohort and fellow research geek Lisa Goodfellow, who knows her archives and offers wise advice in matters great and small.

Thanks to Schwartz & Wade for embracing this book and to Ann Kelley, editor extraordinaire, whose meticulous vision and enthusiasm for *Little Women* and for Louisa May Alcott as a character guided the project from the beginning. I'm grateful also to eagle-eyed copy editors Bara MacNeill and Colleen Fellingham, and to Anne-Marie Varga for assisting. Rachael Cole let me go down a visual rabbit hole, and her talented art direction and design pulled it all together oh so beautifully.

Thanks to Nancy Diessner and Liz Chalfin of Zea Mays Printmaking in Florence, Massachusetts, for patient art inspiration at the outset. Sometimes the simplest solution really is the best.

Finally, thanks to the many writers, researchers, and archives I relied on to retell the story of the Alcotts, with a special shout-out to John Matteson, Harriet Reisen, and Eve LaPlante, and to Houghton Library; Fruitlands Museum curator Shana Dumont Garr, who helped with an impromptu photo shoot, among other things; Jessica Steytler of Concord Free Public Library; and Jan Turnquist, executive director of Louisa May Alcott's Orchard House, for sharing stories in Louisa's owlish room and in the Alcott study.

Picture Captions & Credits

Chapter 1
Photograph by Deborah Noyes

Chapter 2
The opening of Bronson Alcott's controversial *How Like an Angel Came I Down: Conversations with Children on the Gospels* (1836).
Houghton Library, Harvard University

Chapter 3
A page of Bronson Alcott's writings with his daughters' hand- and footprints traced over.
Houghton Library, Harvard University

Chapter 4
A replica of Bronson Alcott's bust of Socrates, courtesy of Fruitlands Museum, The Trustees.
Photograph by Deborah Noyes

Chapter 5
Walden Pond, Concord, Massachusetts.
Library of Congress Prints and Photographs Division, LC-DIG-det-4a18296

Chapter 6
Bronson Alcott's 1840 letter to his mother announcing the family's move to Dove Cottage in Concord, Massachusetts.
Houghton Library, Harvard University

Chapter 7
The Fruitlands farmhouse, Harvard, Massachusetts, courtesy of Fruitlands Museum, The Trustees.
Photograph by Deborah Noyes

Chapter 8
Henry David Thoreau (1856).
Daguerreotype by Benjamin D. Maxham
National Portrait Gallery, Smithsonian Institution

Chapter 9

Page of Louisa May Alcott's handwritten first novel, *The Inheritance*, written when she was a teenager and never published, courtesy of Houghton Library, Harvard University.

Photograph by Deborah Noyes

Chapter 10

Walpole, New Hampshire, playbill announcing Louisa May Alcott and Anna Alcott in starring roles, courtesy of Houghton Library, Harvard University.

Photograph by Deborah Noyes

Chapter 11

Orchard House, Concord, Massachusetts, courtesy of Louisa May Alcott's Orchard House.

Photograph by Deborah Noyes

Chapter 12

Radical abolitionist John Brown (c. 1846).

Daguerreotype by Augustus Washington—National Portrait Gallery, Smithsonian Institution—purchased with major acquisition funds and with funds donated by Betty Adler Schermer in honor of her great-grandfather August M. Bondi

Chapter 13

Tintype of a Union drummer boy from the Civil War, taken between 1861 and 1865.

Library of Congress Prints and Photographs Division, LC-DIG-ppmsca-39546

Chapter 14

A masthead and a sensational etching from *Frank Leslie's Illustrated Newspaper*. In the 1860s, Louisa contributed regular potboilers or "blood and thunder" tales to Leslie's publications.

Banner: Collection of the author

Etching: Hart Picture Archive, Vol. 1

Chapter 15

The Avenue des Champs-Élysées, one of the sights Louisa saw with Laddie during a romantic two-week stay in Paris.

Library of Congress Prints and Photographs Division, LC-DIG-pga-04306

Chapter 16

Cover of *Merry's Museum*, an illustrated magazine for children. Between 1867 and 1870, in addition to writing, Louisa edited and contributed to the magazine.

Courtesy of Pat Pflieger

Notes

The first-edition title page from *Little Women* superimposed over Louisa's handwritten manuscript page.

Text of manuscript page from *Little Women:* Concord Free Library

Little Women title page: Wikimedia Commons

Bibliography

Alcott, Abigail May. *My Heart Is Boundless: Writings of Abigail May Alcott, Louisa's Mother.* Edited by Eve LaPlante. New York: Free Press, 2012.

Alcott, Amos Bronson. *How Like an Angel Came I Down: Conversations with Children on the Gospels.* New York: Lindesfarne Books, 1991.

Alcott, Louisa May. *Alternative Alcott.* Edited by Elaine Showalter. New Brunswick, NJ: Rutgers University Press, 1988.

Alcott, Louisa May. *Aunt Jo's Scrap Bag, vol. 1.* Boston: Roberts Brothers, 1872.

Alcott, Louisa May. *The Journals of Louisa May Alcott.* Edited by Joel Myerson, Daniel Shealy, and Madeleine B. Stern. Athens: University of Georgia Press, 1997.

Alcott, Louisa May. *Little Women.* Edited by Elaine Showalter. New York: Viking Penguin Books, 1989.

Alcott, Louisa May. *Louisa May Alcott: Life, Letters, and Journals.* Edited by Ednah D. Cheney. Boston: Little, Brown, and Company, 1898.

Alcott, Louisa May. *Louisa May Alcott Unmasked: The Collected Thrillers.* Edited by Madeleine B. Stern. Boston: Northeastern University Press, 1995.

Alcott, Louisa May. *Moods.* New Brunswick, NJ: Rutgers University Press, 1991.

Alcott, Louisa May. "Poppy's Pranks." FullReads. http://fullreads.com/literature /poppys-pranks/.

Alcott, Louisa May. *The Selected Letters of Louisa May Alcott.* Edited by Joel Myerson, Daniel Shealy, and Madeleine B. Stern. Athens: University of Georgia Press, 1995.

Alcott, Louisa May. *Work: A Story of Experience.* New York: Penguin, 1994.

Bassett, John Spencer. *A Short History of the United States.* New York: Macmillan, 1915.

Cheever, Susan. *Louisa May Alcott: A Personal Biography.* New York: Simon & Schuster, 2010.

Francis, Richard. *Fruitlands: The Alcott Family and Their Search for Utopia.* New Haven, CT: Yale University Press, 2010.

Lane, Charles. "The Consociate Family Life." *The New Age, Concordium Gazette, & Temperance Advocate,* vol. 1 (August 1843), 116–20.

LaPlante, Eve. *Marmee and Louisa: The Untold Story of Louisa May Alcott and Her Mother.* New York: Simon & Schuster, 2012.

Matteson, John. *Eden's Outcasts: The Story of Louisa May Alcott and Her Father.* New York: W. W. Norton & Company, 2007.

Peabody, Elizabeth Palmer. *Record of a School: Exemplifying the General Principles of Spiritual Culture.* Boston: James Munroe and Company, 1835.

Reisen, Harriet. *Louisa May Alcott: The Woman Behind* Little Women. New York: Picador, 2009.

Saxton, Martha. *Louisa May Alcott: A Modern Biography.* New York: Farrar, Straus and Giroux, 1995.

Shealy, Daniel. *Alcott in Her Own Time: A Biographical Chronicle of Her Life, Drawn from Recollections, Interviews, and Memoirs by Family, Friends, and Associates.* Iowa City: University of Iowa Press, 2005.

Stern, Madeleine B. *Louisa May Alcott: From Blood & Thunder to Hearth & Home.* Boston: Northeastern University Press, 1998.

Thoreau, Henry David. "A Plea for Captain John Brown." UShistory.org. https://www.ushistory.org/documents/thoreau.htm.

Notes

Epigraph

From her father . . . each other: Louisa May Alcott, *Moods,* 84.

I. The Forbidden–Apple Experiment

She has withstood . . . without a struggle: Saxton, *Alcott: A Modern Biography,* 92.

"On a dismal . . . long fight": Louisa May Alcott, *Selected Letters,* 14.

"sprightly, merry . . . every sound": Abigail Alcott, *My Heart Is Boundless,* 48.

"A child is . . . paths of truth": Matteson, *Eden's Outcasts,* 43.

"must not be repeated": Matteson, 45.

"history . . . faithfully narrated": Matteson, 44.

"vivid, energetic": Reisen, *Woman Behind* Little Women, 20.

"lives and moves and breathes": Saxton, *Alcott: A Modern Biography,* 77.

"the wild exuberance . . . scuffle of things": Matteson, *Eden's Outcasts,* 49.

"most confirmed habits": Reisen, *Woman Behind* Little Women, 24.

"in a state of excitement" through "deter me": Saxton, *Alcott: A Modern Biography,* 79.

"Should little girls" through "spiritual principle": Saxton, 90–92.

"not deeply interested . . . moral subjects": Saxton, 78.

"continued at . . . of success": Abigail Alcott, *My Heart Is Boundless,* 45.

2. Queen of the Revel

My father taught . . . could digest: Louisa May Alcott, *Her Life, Letters, and Journals,* 29.

"amazed": Matteson, *Eden's Outcasts,* 56.

"genius for education": Matteson, 56.

"Every face was eager and interested": Peabody, *Record of a School,* 2.

"Mr. Alcott sat . . . children themselves": Peabody, 2.

"animal": Matteson, *Eden's Outcasts,* 40.

"The child has . . . to govern": Matteson, 45.

"profound and deep stillness": Peabody, *Record of a School,* 145.

"She is very fond" through "craved bread": Abigail Alcott, *My Heart Is Boundless,* 71.

"Two little girls" through "picture back again": Saxton, *Alcott: A Modern Biography,* 83–84.

"apt and fit questions": Amos Bronson Alcott, *How Like an Angel,* 266.

"It has a little head" through "love me . . . little sister": Reisen, *Woman Behind* Little Women, 38.

"A teacher should . . . his own": Peabody, *Record of a School,* 19.

"the true teacher . . . self-trust": Matteson, *Eden's Outcasts,* 93.

"The cakes fell short" through "noble life": Louisa May Alcott, *Her Life, Letters, and Journals,* 27.

3. Without Compass or Chart

This reminds me . . . for gingerbread: Abigail Alcott, *My Heart Is Boundless,* 72–73.

"kindle a fire for the mind": Cheever, *A Personal Biography,* 6.

"seize the happiest" through "Louisa intentionally": Saxton, *Alcott: A Modern Biography,* 88.

"who from the mere . . . for protection": Reisen, *Woman Behind* Little Women, 32–33.

"In moods of quiet" through "part of speech": Reisen, 25.

"Anna says . . . cheek so": Matteson, *Eden's Outcasts,* 65.

"Could I have . . . Not so Louisa": Saxton, *Alcott: A Modern Biography,* 89.

"One builds . . . demolishes": Matteson, *Eden's Outcasts,* 64.

"Louisa and Anna . . . from an encounter": Saxton, *Alcott: A Modern Biography,* 89.

"ferocity" through "at times alarming": Reisen, *Woman Behind* Little Women, 33.

"impromptu picnics" through "a big Newfoundland": Shealy, *Alcott in Her Own Time,* 33.

"impetuous stream . . . compass or chart": Reisen, *Woman Behind* Little Women, 39.

"signs of impending evil": Matteson, *Eden's Outcasts,* 10.

"inadequacy of maternal culture": Matteson, 74.

"offensively assertive": Matteson, 75.

4. Poor as Rats

I have often . . . grown-up people: Amos Bronson Alcott, *How Like an Angel,* 12.

"naughtiness": Matteson, *Eden's Outcasts,* 77.

"Mrs. Alcott came . . . read them": Reisen, *Woman Behind* Little Women, 36.

"absurd . . . half-witted": Matteson, *Eden's Outcasts,* 80.

"blasphemy": Matteson, 12.

"the adult mind" through "barking at you": Matteson, 81.

"not a single . . . great purpose": Matteson, 12.

"unbroken silence": Matteson, 82.

"You have seen . . . injured one": Abigail Alcott, *My Heart Is Boundless,* 75.

"Go away . . . father unhappy": Matteson, *Eden's Outcasts,* 10.

"to whom I clung . . . her cry": Louisa May Alcott, *Aunt Jo's Scrap Bag,* 2–4.

"a deer or . . . in a race": LaPlante, *Marmee and Louisa,* 91.

"I did something" through "the broken friendship": Louisa May Alcott, *Aunt Jo's Scrap Bag,* 3.

"revenged": Louisa May Alcott, *Aunt Jo's Scrap Bag,* 4.

"the dismissal . . . decline": Matteson, *Eden's Outcasts,* 84.

"We are poor as rats": Abigail Alcott, *My Heart Is Boundless,* 80.

"the Hoper": Reisen, *Woman Behind* Little Women, 47.

"Don't distress yourself . . . concern him": Matteson, *Eden's Outcasts,* 36.

"been through a good deal . . ." through . . . "mournful object": Louisa May Alcott, "Poppy's Pranks," 7.

"his own spade": Reisen, *Woman Behind* Little Women, 57.

"always GOOD": Reisen, *Woman Behind* Little Women, 53.

5. The Little Kingdom

She wasn't a . . . feared nothing: Louisa May Alcott, "Poppy's Pranks," 1.

"in rapture": Reisen, *Woman Behind* Little Women, 55.

"Father told us . . . complain sometimes": Matteson, *Eden's Outcasts,* 88.

"leader in the fun" and "higher than her head": Reisen, *Woman Behind* Little Women, 59.

"Cy was a comrade . . ." through ". . . haunt me yet": Louisa May Alcott, *Aunt Jo's Scrap Bag,* 8–9.

"wanted to romp . . . riot about": Louisa May Alcott, "Poppy's Pranks," 6.

"Our giant came . . . squash vine": Reisen, *Woman Behind* Little Women, 59.

"all that farmers . . ." through ". . . own heart": Matteson, *Eden's Outcasts,* 91.

"any more than . . . come to him": Reisen, *Woman Behind* Little Women, 56.

"massive head . . . all disguises": Louisa May Alcott, *Moods,* 36.

"still water . . . condition of life": Matteson, *Eden's Outcasts,* 89.

"one of the dullest . . . in Massachusetts": Louisa May Alcott, *Selected Letters,* 127.

"topsey-turvey": Louisa May Alcott, *The Journals,* 73.

A little kingdom . . . governing it well: Reisen, *Woman Behind* Little Women, 123.

"two devils . . . her daughter": Matteson, *Eden's Outcasts,* 189.

"part of one . . . at a time": Louisa May Alcott, *Little Women,* ix.

"Two [children] make peace": LaPlante, *Marmee and Louisa,* 94.

My Dear Louisa . . . Your Father: Reisen, *Woman Behind* Little Women, 61.

"longed to see mamma" through ". . . danger was the fun": Louisa May Alcott, "Poppy's Pranks," 6.

6. "What Makes Me So Happy?"

A philosopher . . . him down: Louisa May Alcott, *Her Life, Letters, and Journals,* 315.

"My baby . . . her genius": Abigail Alcott, *My Heart Is Boundless,* 83.

"lucky": Louisa May Alcott, *The Journals,* 105.

"If it would . . ." through ". . . trot and canter": Abigail Alcott, *My Heart Is Boundless,* 84.

"My father did not love me": Reisen, *Woman Behind* Little Women, 65.

"My girls shall have trades": Abigail Alcott, *My Heart Is Boundless,* 88.

"in another person's yoke": Abigail Alcott, 87.

"great firmness . . . and desponding": Abigail Alcott, 106.

"Why . . . Give!": Abigail Alcott, 92.

"My dear brother . . . to be done?": Abigail Alcott, 88.

"plies her hands . . . the garden": Reisen, *Woman Behind* Little Women, 67.

"did not dare . . . crave it": Francis, *Fruitlands,* 62.

"hovel": Francis, 63.

"I believe he . . . necessarily implicated": Matteson, *Eden's Outcasts,* 96.

"pick-bones and cranberry sauce": Abigail Alcott, *My Heart Is Boundless,* 81.

"My children . . . generous and fearless": Abigail Alcott, 93.

"talk, talk, talk": Reisen, *Woman Behind* Little Women, 63.

"a tedious archangel": Matteson, *Eden's Outcasts,* 69.

"serene and lofty": Cheever, *A Personal Biography,* 49.

"He will not . . . nervous excitation": Francis, *Fruitlands,* 65.

"Here is a . . . deal with": Reisen, *Woman Behind* Little Women, 70.

"quite ready . . . into practice": Reisen, 71.

"wife, children . . . to realize": Abigail Alcott, *My Heart Is Boundless,* 98.

A picture for you . . . grouped together: Abigail Alcott, 117.

"It is with . . . bark alone": Abigail Alcott, 96.

"hardships, doubt . . . disgrace": Abigail Alcott, 95.

"I am enjoying . . . fortify me": Abigail Alcott, 104.

"I have not . . . precious to me": Matteson, *Eden's Outcasts,* 103.

"I live, move . . . in them": Abigail Alcott, *My Heart Is Boundless*, 102.

"I seldom . . . each other": Abigail Alcott, 106.

"consociate family": Matteson, *Eden's Outcasts*, 106.

"Good news . . ." through ". . . me so happy?" Abigail Alcott, *My Heart Is Boundless*, 112.

"atmosphere of restriction . . ." through "suffocation": Abigail Alcott, 113.

"I live, my dear . . . proud, discomfort": Reisen, *Woman Behind* Little Women, 79.

"pure poetic fire": Reisen, 124.

"DEAR DAUGHTER . . . do good": LaPlante, *Marmee and Louisa*, 107.

"toil-worn and depressed": Abigail Alcott, *My Heart Is Boundless*, 115.

"arduous and involved duties": Abigail Alcott, 114.

"We may be . . . some weeks": LaPlante, *Marmee and Louisa*, 107.

"bounteous stores": Reisen, *Woman Behind* Little Women, 80.

"quickened by . . . and love": Abigail Alcott, *My Heart Is Boundless*, 115.

"Give me one day . . . and discussion": Abigail Alcott, 114.

"Providence": LaPlante, *Marmee and Louisa*, 115.

"no one can . . . without loving": Reisen, *Woman Behind* Little Women, 73.

"I would as soon . . . a madman": Francis, *Fruitlands*, 99.

"whole doctrine . . . land & money": Francis, 106.

"You ask too much": Francis, 105.

"I hope the . . . my mind": Abigail Alcott, *My Heart Is Boundless*, 114.

"eventful": Abigail Alcott, 117.

7. The Pathetic Family

And here his wife . . . her children: Louisa May Alcott, *Alternative Alcott*, 366.

"the bowl of Heaven": Cheever, *A Personal Biography*, 64.

"in two plates . . . one mug": Reisen, *Woman Behind* Little Women, 88.

"our little territory . . ." through ". . . such a region": LaPlante, *Marmee and Louisa*, 112.

"the true men . . ." through ". . . have dared": Abigail Alcott, *My Heart Is Boundless*, 118.

"simplicity in diet . . . serene minds": Lane, "The Consociate Family Life," 116.

"English mystics": Francis, *Fruitlands*, 113.

"Vegetable diet . . . nightmare": Louisa May Alcott, *The Journals*, 47.

"I rose at five . . . cold water!": Louisa May Alcott, *The Journals*, 45.

"schoolboy, dilettante spiritualism": Reisen, *Woman Behind* Little Women, 94.

"see what would come of it": Matteson, *Eden's Outcasts*, 125.

"They look well . . . December": Matteson, 139.

"I like the farm . . . Mr. Lane": Louisa May Alcott, *The Journals*, 47.

"were sheltered under our roof": Reisen, *Woman Behind* Little Women, 202.

"over a thousand . . . reach Canada": LaPlante, *Marmee and Louisa*, 131.

"We had a dinner of bread and water": Louisa May Alcott, *The Journals*, 44.

"the yoke on woman": Abigail Alcott, *My Heart Is Boundless*, 124.

"Only one woman!": Louisa May Alcott, *Alternative Alcott*, 373.

"the Pathetic Family": Louisa May Alcott, *The Journals*, 85.

"I get to sleep . . . family this day": Louisa May Alcott, *The Journals*, 45–46.

"I was cross . . . very bad": Louisa May Alcott, *The Journals*, 45.

TO MOTHER . . . cherish thee: LaPlante, *Marmee and Louisa*, 259.

"the best woman in the world": Louisa May Alcott, *The Journals*, 55.

"a most loving disposition towards us": Abigail Alcott, *My Heart Is Boundless*, 123.

"Visited the Shakers . . . form or another": Abigail Alcott, 124.

"Though it was . . . happy within": Louisa May Alcott, *The Journals*, 43.

"No one will . . . Mother": Louisa May Alcott, *The Journals*, 46.

"I had a music . . . so fussy": Louisa May Alcott, *The Journals*, 45.

"groan lamentably . . . been in one": Louisa May Alcott, *Alternative Alcott*, 371.

"sad lapse from virtue": Louisa May Alcott, *Alternative Alcott*, 373.

"peculiar maternal love . . . all else": LaPlante, *Marmee and Louisa*, 114.

"the very mischief": Matteson, *Eden's Outcasts*, 156.

"Father and Mr. L. . . . she is so tired": Louisa May Alcott, *The Journals*, 47.

"a Hotel where man . . ." through ". . . to love": Abigail Alcott, *My Heart Is Boundless*, 125.

"I mean to take my cubs and escape": Francis, *Fruitlands*, 260.

"Mr. L was . . . keep us together": Louisa May Alcott, *The Journals*, 47.

"Mr. Lane's efforts . . . strong": LaPlante, *Marmee and Louisa*, 129.

"My faithful wife . . . dwarfed and killed": Matteson, *Eden's Outcasts*, 162.

I wrote in my Imagination Book . . . it was happy: Louisa May Alcott, *The Journals*, 51.

8. *The Model Children*

We are dreadfull . . . think of: Louisa May Alcott, *Selected Letters*, 4.

"quite comfortable . . . quarters": Abigail Alcott, *My Heart Is Boundless*, 129.

"the brain . . . common concerns": Matteson, *Eden's Outcasts*, 167.

"I scarcely . . . begin": Saxton, *Alcott: A Modern Biography*, 156.

"an asylum . . . to the strong": Matteson, *Eden's Outcasts*, 169.

"Our home is humble . . ." through "pranks": Reisen, *Woman Behind* Little Women, 108–9.

"got mad, she could be severe": Shealy, *Alcott in Her Own Time*, 121.

"We christened . . ." through ". . . to matured fruit": Reisen, *Woman Behind* Little Women, 109–11.

"full of life . . . nervous": Reisen, 3.

"like a gazelle" through "girl runner": Reisen, 3.

"Mr. A's inclinations . . . Concord": Reisen, 111.

"I dread his falling . . . view in sight": Abigail Alcott, *My Heart Is Boundless*, 134.

"More people . . . no one else": Louisa May Alcott, *The Journals*, 56.

"love of cats": Louisa May Alcott, *The Journals*, 55.

"write on the hearth with charcoal": Reisen, *Woman Behind* Little Women, 202.

"an amiable, intelligent . . . Bondage": Abigail Alcott, *My Heart Is Boundless*, 149.

"thirty years old . . . dire entity of slavery": Reisen, *Woman Behind* Little Women, 202.

"strange combination . . . friend beware": Reisen, 4.

"write something great . . ." through ". . . magnificent boots": Reisen, 117.

"a beautiful walk . . . like crazy folks": Louisa May Alcott, *Selected Letters*, 4.

"indolent . . . impotence": Abigail Alcott, *My Heart Is Boundless*, 140.

"the happiest of my life" through ". . . model children, Miss Fuller": Shealy, *Alcott in Her Own Time*, 35.

"romantic . . . sleeping quietly": Cheever, *A Personal Biography*, 83.

"master": Shealy, *Alcott in Her Own Time*, 36.

"natural source . . . their angels": Reisen, *Woman Behind* Little Women, 130.

"at once fired with the desire . . . scared me to bed": Shealy, *Alcott in Her Own Time*, 36.

"the genius of the wood": Reisen, *Woman Behind* Little Women, 226.

"I have at last . . ." through ". . . like sanctuary": Louisa May Alcott, *The Journals,* 59.

"what no books can teach": LaPlante, *Marmee and Louisa,* 92.

"I stood there . . . all my life": Louisa May Alcott, *The Journals,* 57.

"Your temperament . . . really help you": Abigail Alcott, *My Heart Is Boundless,* 147.

"a safety valve . . . tender heart": Abigail Alcott, 138.

"May this pen . . . the best": Abigail Alcott, 146.

"I am sure . . . sure to come": Abigail Alcott, 147.

"MY DEAREST LOUY . . . your MOTHER": Louisa May Alcott, *The Journals,* 55.

"I don't see . . . poor now": Louisa May Alcott, *The Journals,* 56.

"not insane . . . paying our debts": Abigail Alcott, *My Heart Is Boundless,* 145–46.

"retirement . . . provident care": Abigail Alcott, 160.

"It seems a great . . . live again": Reisen, *Woman Behind* Little Women, 130.

"an anxious counsel" through ". . . see if I won't!": Shealy, *Alcott in Her Own Time,* 37.

"trials of life . . . childhood ended": Shealy, 36.

9. *"Stick to Your Teaching" & Other Dramatic Interludes*

I won't teach . . . I'll prove it: Louisa May Alcott, *The Journals,* 109.

"poor as rats . . . Lord": Louisa May Alcott, *The Journals,* 65.

"I try not . . ." through ". . . to find it": Louisa May Alcott, *The Journals,* 61.

"a missionary to the poor": LaPlante, *Marmee and Louisa,* 151.

"I have taken . . . must decide": Abigail Alcott, *My Heart Is Boundless,* 154.

"I can't talk . . . add any more": Louisa May Alcott, *The Journals,* 62.

"quiet days . . . doing to us?": Abigail Alcott, *My Heart Is Boundless,* 155–56.

"I felt like . . . sea-gull": Shealy, *Alcott in Her Own Time,* 37.

"feeble and homesick" through ". . . But waiting is so *hard!*": Louisa May Alcott, *The Journals,* 63.

"the cold neglect . . . desire to help us": Abigail Alcott, *My Heart Is Boundless,* 136.

"a gloomy glare": Shealy, *Alcott in Her Own Time,* 38.

"Anna wants to be . . ." through "Mother says wait": Louisa May Alcott, *The Journals,* 14.

"I don't *talk* . . ." through ". . . done something": Louisa May Alcott, *The Journals,* 61–62.

"peacemaker . . . beloved of all": Matteson, *Eden's Outcasts,* 197.

"I often think . . . before I can do it": Louisa May Alcott, *The Journals,* 63.

"had the truest . . . significance of life": Matteson, *Eden's Outcasts,* 200.

"in a blaze of being": Matteson, 201.

"heartless . . . let it not be so": Matteson, 203.

"Peace fills his breast": Matteson, 204.

"intelligence office": Matteson, 198.

Best American . . . Mrs. Alcott's rooms: Reisen, *Woman Behind* Little Women, 143.

"Some poor immigrants . . . one day": Louisa May Alcott, *The Journals,* 31.

"Father and mother . . . sympathy, help": Louisa May Alcott, *The Journals,* 67.

"I shall be . . . thing happens": Louisa May Alcott, *The Journals,* 65.

"My life . . . abuses of Society": Matteson, *Eden's Outcasts,* 212.

"service in the country . . . I am ready": Abigail Alcott, *My Heart Is Boundless,* 180.

"system of servitude": Matteson, *Eden's Outcasts,* 212.

"always did what . . ." through ". . . wicked men": Louisa May Alcott, *The Journals,* 67.

"timid mouse . . . sentimental rubbish": Reisen, *Woman Behind* Little Women, 146.

"important and admired": Matteson, *Eden's Outcasts,* 215.

"a half-frozen wanderer" through ". . . lesson in real love": Louisa May Alcott, *The Journals*, 71.

"Still at High St. . . . Hard times for all": Louisa May Alcott, *The Journals*, 68.

"Stick to your teaching . . . can't write": Louisa May Alcott, *The Journals*, 109.

"Mothers are always . . . first-born": Louisa May Alcott, *The Journals*, 73.

"Whatever beauty . . ." through "no matter how empty": Louisa May Alcott, *Selected Letters*, 11–12.

10. Battering Ram

I took my . . . for my failures: Louisa May Alcott, *The Journals*, 79.

"quiet": Louisa May Alcott, *Letters*, 15.

"no dramatic genius . . . a great one": Reisen, *Woman Behind* Little Women, 162.

"Sewing won't . . . down on Sundays": Louisa May Alcott, *The Journals*, 78.

"I am trying . . . by stories": Louisa May Alcott, *Selected Letters*, 14.

"an anxious time": Matteson, *Eden's Outcasts*, 227.

"a nice stupid winter": Matteson, 225.

"a dark . . . propriety": Reisen, *Woman Behind* Little Women, 167.

"sent into life . . . the programme": Reisen, 173.

"[I have] a queer . . . my private benefit": Louisa May Alcott, *Selected Letters*, 18.

"swarming up . . . of Walpole": Louisa May Alcott, *Selected Letters*, 19.

"as money is . . . my bow": Louisa May Alcott, *Selected Letters*, 16.

"experiment to be independent . . . busy head": Louisa May Alcott, *Selected Letters*, 21.

"I can go . . ." through ". . . good will and sympathy": Louisa May Alcott, *Selected Letters*, 19–20.

"I think I shall" through "support myself": Louisa May Alcott, *Selected Letters*, 26.

"sending money home . . . independence better": Louisa May Alcott, *The Journals*, 81–82.

"I clutched it . . ." through ". . . fortune in prospect": Louisa May Alcott, *Selected Letters*, 28–30.

"a house needs . . ." through ". . . much for this world": Louisa May Alcott, *The Journals*, 85.

"the case is a critical one": Reisen, *Woman Behind* Little Women, 175.

"neither flesh nor strength to spare . . ." "continuance": Matteson, 231.

"He is never happy . . . helps him": Louisa May Alcott, *The Journals*, 85.

"do more for . . . known to me": Matteson, *Eden's Outcasts*, 232.

11. The First Break

Give me . . . willing feet: Reisen, *Woman Behind* Little Women, 174.

"I have done . . ." through ". . . to live in it": Louisa May Alcott, *The Journals*, 85–86.

"Apple Slump": Louisa May Alcott, *The Journals*, 93.

"dear Betty . . . patient as always": Louisa May Alcott, *The Journals*, 85.

"wasted to . . . she was": Matteson, *Eden's Outcasts*, 235.

"my boy": Louisa May Alcott, *Selected Letters*, 37.

"Twenty-five this month . . . when I am near": Louisa May Alcott, *The Journals*, 86.

"I entered the house . . . out of the room": Reisen, *Woman Behind* Little Women, 177.

"will be something new . . . spared of the four": Matteson, *Eden's Outcasts*, 235.

"For two days she suffered . . . not liking Concord": Louisa May Alcott, *The Journals*, 88–89.

"I have plans . . . see my way": Louisa May Alcott, *The Journals*, 90.

"a model son . . . fine possibility": Louisa May Alcott, *The Journals*, 89.

"Slough of Despond": Louisa May Alcott, *The Journals*, 69.

"find interest in something . . ." through ". . . manage them alone": Louisa May Alcott, *The Journals*, 90–91.

"all the nooks . . . unexpected places": Reisen, *Woman Behind* Little Women, 182.

"wandering family . . ." through ". . . just now": Louisa May Alcott, *The Journals*, 90.

"Last week was . . . at the water": Louisa May Alcott, *Selected Letters*, 34.

"bonny bride" through ". . . through the night": Louisa May Alcott, *Work,* 122–24.

"My fit of despair . . ." through ". . . Louisa will succeed": Louisa May Alcott, *The Journals*, 90–91.

"bore herself . . . great pleasure": Reisen, *Woman Behind* Little Women, 185.

"This past year . . ." through ". . . darken my soul": Louisa May Alcott, *The Journals*, 91–92.

"invest . . . Sinking Fund": Louisa May Alcott, *Selected Letters,* 38.

"Abby [May] & I . . . her 'shining hours'": Louisa May Alcott, *Selected Letters,* 44.

"run up and warm . . . many fireplaces": Matteson, *Eden's Outcasts,* 247.

"Dear man! . . . his wisdom!": Louisa May Alcott, *The Journals,* 92.

"the house joyous": Matteson, *Eden's Outcasts,* 247.

"I am spending . . . little jollifications": Louisa May Alcott, *Selected Letters,* 40.

"Wonder if I ought . . ." through ". . . campaign ends well": Louisa May Alcott, *The Journals,* 94.

12. Boiling Over

To and fro . . . swept over her: Louisa May Alcott, *Unmasked,* 3.

"These men are . . . action—action!": Bassett, *A Short History of the United States,* 502.

"the public practice of humanity": Matteson, *Eden's Outcasts,* 252.

"We are boiling over . . . not set right soon": Louisa May Alcott, *Selected Letters,* 49.

"I am here . . . his immortal life": Thoreau, UShistory.org. https://www.ushistory.org/documents /thoreau.htm.

"A meeting . . ." through ". . . I can nurse": Louisa May Alcott, *The Journals,* 26.

"I felt much . . . and very happy": Louisa May Alcott, *The Journals,* 95.

"natural dignity": Louisa May Alcott, *Selected Letters,* 55.

"The dear girl . . ." through ". . . picture to remember": Louisa May Alcott, *The Journals,* 99.

"putting a small . . . memory inviolate": Reisen, *Woman Behind* Little Women, 192.

"bereaved family . . . baked meats": Louisa May Alcott, *Selected Letters,* 54.

"haunt[ing] the road . . . hat off": Louisa May Alcott, *The Journals,* 98.

"the wise mother . . . self-sacrifice": Louisa May Alcott, *Her Life, Letters, and Journals,* 94.

"I have decided . . . L.M. Alcott": Reisen, *Woman Behind* Little Women, 193.

"where she and her mate . . ." through ". . . friend by him": Louisa May Alcott, *The Journals,* 99.

"Mr. H is . . . clutch him": Louisa May Alcott, *Selected Letters,* 54.

"a worthy boy . . . rods and fun": Louisa May Alcott, *Selected Letters,* 57.

"vortex . . . cross, or despondent": Reisen, *Woman Behind* Little Women, 198.

"Genius burned . . ." through ". . . patriot than poet": Reisen, 194–96.

"She is not wanting . . . certainly joins": Matteson, *Eden's Outcasts,* 259.

"A quiet Christmas . . . Mother says, '. . . sugar plums'": Louisa May Alcott, *The Journals,* 101.

13. Owling

Being fond . . . the night: Louisa May Alcott, *Alternative Alcott,* 32.

"I corked . . . turned nurse": Louisa May Alcott, *The Journals,* 103.

"possessed": Louisa May Alcott, *The Journals,* 99.

"his reddest apples . . ." through ". . . Lu's first novel": Louisa May Alcott, *The Journals,* 102–4.

"They are no judges": Stern, *From Blood & Thunder,* 214.

"a story that touches . . . characters do?" Matteson, *Eden's Outcasts,* 300.

"I think disappointment . . . before I die": Louisa May Alcott, *The Journals*, 105.

"poke each other's . . . most valiantly": Matteson, *Eden's Outcasts*, 264.

"fly at some body": Louisa May Alcott, *Selected Letters*, 65.

"In a little town . . . times like these": Louisa May Alcott, *The Journals*, 105.

"sewing violently . . . blue shirts": Louisa May Alcott, *Selected Letters*, 64.

"wrote, read . . . something to do": Louisa May Alcott, *The Journals*, 106.

"There is no . . . at present": Louisa May Alcott, *Selected Letters*, 65.

"in style . . . clever people": Matteson, *Eden's Outcasts*, 266.

"Hate to visit" through "hair to do it": Louisa May Alcott, *The Journals*, 108–9.

"failing and feeble": Matteson, *Eden's Outcasts*, 267.

"Henry would not . . ." through ". . . the solemn change": Louisa May Alcott, *Selected Letters*, 74–75.

"I saw . . . a tall, thin . . ." through ". . . see you, as I did": Shealy, *Alcott in Her Own Time*, 124.

"Davis said . . . each did so": Louisa May Alcott, *The Journals*, 109.

"I intend to . . . this 'The Maniac . . . tale of passion'": Louisa May Alcott, *Selected Letters*, 79.

"rubbishy": Louisa May Alcott, *The Journals*, 139.

"that class . . . have a holiday": Louisa May Alcott, *Unmasked*, xii.

"To have had . . . armor of propriety": Louisa May Alcott, *Little Women*, xii.

"I think my . . . before the public": Louisa May Alcott, *Unmasked*, xiv.

"I long to . . . who can": Louisa May Alcott, *The Journals*, 105.

"pent-up energy . . ." through ". . . thank Heaven!": Louisa May Alcott, *The Journals*, 110.

"If you intend . . . mend you up": Louisa May Alcott, *Selected Letters*, 82.

"I was ready . . . I marched": Louisa May Alcott, *The Journals*, 110.

"I have a . . . while I packed": Louisa May Alcott, *Alternative Alcott*, 5.

"Shall I stay?" through ". . . old face again?": Reisen, *Woman Behind* Little Women, 210.

"set forth . . ." through ". . . courage and plans": Louisa May Alcott, *The Journals*, 110.

"blow up . . . my destiny": Reisen, *Woman Behind* Little Women, 210–11.

"like snow . . . warm ground": Matteson, *Eden's Outcasts*, 273.

"rolling in . . . great gate": Reisen, *Woman Behind* Little Women, 211.

"The Hurly-burly House . . . from home": Louisa May Alcott, *Alternative Alcott*, 18.

"We are cheered . . . out of bed": Matteson, *Eden's Outcasts*, 272.

"pneumonia on one side . . ." through ". . . their tortured bodies": Louisa May Alcott, *Alternative Alcott*, 21.

"You are real . . . comfort everyone": Matteson, *Eden's Outcasts*, 274.

"manfully": Louisa May Alcott, *Alternative Alcott*, 23.

"the poor souls . . . accomplished seamstress": Louisa May Alcott, *Alternative Alcott*, 29.

"washy": Louisa May Alcott, *The Journals*, 114.

"Regards to Plato": Louisa May Alcott, *Selected Letters*, 113.

"given to confidences . . . exceeding young": Louisa May Alcott, *The Journals*, 115.

"a black-eyed widow": Louisa May Alcott, *Alternative Alcott*, 32.

"It was a strange . . . wind instruments": Louisa May Alcott, *Alternative Alcott*, 34.

"duty room . . . pathetic room": Louisa May Alcott, *Alternative Alcott*, 33.

"owling": Louisa May Alcott, *Alternative Alcott*, 32.

"Some grow stern . . . him by day": Louisa May Alcott, *Alternative Alcott*, 34.

"A most attractive . . . secret of content": Louisa May Alcott, *Alternative Alcott*, 39.

"Straightaway my fear . . . 'Thank you . . . I wanted'": Louisa May Alcott, *Alternative Alcott*, 40–41.

"It was John's . . . in his hand": Louisa May Alcott, *Alternative Alcott*, 46.

We, sighing, said . . . "For such . . . no death": Reisen, *Woman Behind* Little Women, 226.

"danced": Matteson, *Eden's Outcasts*, 279.

"I never began . . . I like it": Louisa May Alcott, *The Journals*, 113.

"in their sympathy . . . are mortal": Louisa May Alcott, *Alternative Alcott*, 53.

"Ordered to . . . from home!": Louisa May Alcott, *The Journals*, 115.

"I was learning . . . those about us": Louisa May Alcott, *Alternative Alcott*, 59–60.

"This will end . . ." through ". . . weariness and pain": Matteson, *Eden's Outcasts*, 280–81.

"Dream awfully . . . likely to do": Louisa May Alcott, *The Journals*, 115.

"grey-headed gentleman . . . like a ghost": Matteson, *Eden's Outcasts*, 282.

"Was amazed . . . have to go": Louisa May Alcott, *The Journals*, 116.

"Horrid war" through ". . . I answered 'yes, father'": Matteson, *Eden's Outcasts*, 282.

14. Mercenary Creature

Taking the hint . . . awaited me: Louisa May Alcott, *The Journals*, 124.

"May's shocked face . . ." through ". . . died or got well": Louisa May Alcott, *The Journals*, 116–17.

"enjoyed . . . crazy part": Louisa May Alcott, *The Journals*, 112.

"Poor Louy left . . . made willingly": Reisen, *Woman Behind* Little Women, 221.

"hollow-eyed . . ." through ". . . could not speak": Reisen, 224.

"wouldn't go" through ". . . wouldn't be a girl'": Louisa May Alcott, *The Journals*, 117–18.

"Ever your . . . a bones Lu": Louisa May Alcott, *Selected Letters*, 83.

"beautiful and new" through ". . . one to me": Reisen, *Woman Behind* Little Women, 224.

"witty and sympathetic": Reisen, 116.

"I find . . . without knowing it": Louisa May Alcott, *The Journals*, 122.

"quiet humor . . ." through ". . . poultices to cool": Reisen, *Woman Behind* Little Women, 225.

"Sketches never . . . awaited me": Louisa May Alcott, *The Journals*, 124.

"neighbor Hawthorne": Reisen, *Woman Behind* Little Women, 226.

"Had a fresh . . . the honor": Louisa May Alcott, *The Journals*, 119.

"I can't afford . . . family cosey": Louisa May Alcott, *Her Life, Letters, and Journals*, 165.

"Mr. Leslie . . . such sacrifice": Louisa May Alcott, *Unmasked*, xv.

"All my dreams . . . 'stick to her teaching'": Louisa May Alcott, *The Journals*, 121.

"to flavor . . . fair ladies": Louisa May Alcott, *Selected Letters*, 93.

"I let her . . ." through ". . . proud, I think": Louisa May Alcott, *The Journals*, 131–33.

"I hope success . . . good daughter": Louisa May Alcott, *Selected Letters*, 106.

"The two most . . . the average": Reisen, *Woman Behind* Little Women, 233.

"Moods is . . . I meant": Reisen, 235.

"back on rubbishy tales": Louisa May Alcott, *Her Life, Letters, and Journals*, 165.

"several hundred . . . [her] feelings": Louisa May Alcott, *The Journals*, 132.

"Alcott brains . . ." through "grand jollification": Louisa May Alcott, *The Journals*, 139–40.

"martyr . . . cherished idol": Matteson, *Eden's Outcasts*, 308.

"a fine little . . ." through "long-desired dream": Louisa May Alcott, *The Journals*, 140.

15. Mi Drogha

We led a happy life together: Louisa May Alcott, *Aunt Jo's Scrap Bag*, 27.

"I might not . . ." through "got into a novel": Louisa May Alcott, *The Journals*, 141.

"sat bolt upright . . . asked questions": Reisen, *Woman Behind* Little Women, 238.

"narrow valley . . ." through ". . . all my faults": Louisa May Alcott, *The Journals,* 142–43.

"Who was Goethe": Louisa May Alcott, *The Journals,* 147.

"most romantic": Louisa May Alcott, *The Journals,* 144.

"If only . . . from all quarters of the world": Reisen, *Woman Behind* Little Women, 239.

"overfed": Matteson, *Eden's Outcasts,* 314.

"Col Polk . . . grew very tired": Louisa May Alcott, *The Journals,* 144.

"a tall youth . . ." through ". . . we were friends": Louisa May Alcott, *Aunt Jo's Scrap Bag,* 17–18.

"Ladislas . . . name perfectly": Louisa May Alcott, *Aunt Jo's Scrap Bag,* 16.

"many friends . . ." through "I ever heard": Louisa May Alcott, *Aunt Jo's Scrap Bag,* 18–19.

"*mi drogha* . . . tenderest manner": Louisa May Alcott, *Aunt Jo's Scrap Bag,* 28.

"lonely, poor, and ill": Louisa May Alcott, *Aunt Jo's Scrap Bag,* 18.

"I am imbecile! . . ." through ". . . to write together": Louisa May Alcott, *Aunt Jo's Scrap Bag,* 21–22.

"little romance": Louisa May Alcott, *The Journals,* 145.

"splendid plans for the future": Louisa May Alcott, *Aunt Jo's Scrap Bag,* 22.

"his sweetest airs . . ." through ". . . time goes on": Louisa May Alcott, *The Journals,* 145.

"jokingly agreed . . . '*Bon voyage . . . au revoir*'": Louisa May Alcott, *Aunt Jo's Scrap Bag,* 23.

"disconsolate . . . or interesting": Louisa May Alcott, *The Journals,* 145.

"every one . . . within doors": Louisa May Alcott, *The Journals,* 148.

"Tired of it . . . best apart": Louisa May Alcott, *The Journals,* 150.

"might have been . . . too exciting": Louisa May Alcott, *The Journals,* 149.

"in the best of French" through ". . . spring weather": Louisa May Alcott, *Aunt Jo's Scrap Bag,* 26–27.

"ran away . . . had given me": Louisa May Alcott, *Aunt Jo's Scrap Bag,* 31.

"the pleasantest . . . year of travel": Louisa May Alcott, *Aunt Jo's Scrap Bag,* 25.

"My twelve . . . quite proper": Louisa May Alcott, *Aunt Jo's Scrap Bag,* 27.

"feeling as if . . . for us": Louisa May Alcott, *Aunt Jo's Scrap Bag,* 31.

"A little romance . . . couldn't be": Louisa May Alcott, *The Journals,* 148.

"We led a happy life": Louisa May Alcott, *Aunt Jo's Scrap Bag,* 27.

10. Never Liked Girls

Wonder if I . . . something yet: Louisa May Alcott, *The Journals,* 85.

"foppish curls . . . worn-out actor": Louisa May Alcott, *The Journals,* 155.

"Get all you . . . world wide influence": Matteson, *Eden's Outcasts,* 324.

"wildly around . . . still here": Louisa May Alcott, *The Journals,* 152–53.

"dread[ed] debt more than the devil": Louisa May Alcott, *The Journals,* 158.

"never expect . . ." through ". . . in three months": Louisa May Alcott, *The Journals,* 154.

"Louisa Alcott . . . full of neuralgia": Reisen, *Woman Behind* Little Women, 255.

"I was never . . . well afterward": Louisa May Alcott, *Her Life, Letters, and Journals,* 138.

"golden goose": a reference to Louisa's poem "The Lay of the Golden Goose," which joked of her unexpected status as family provider.

"Bills accumulate and worry me": Louisa May Alcott, *The Journals,* 158.

"Niles, partner . . ." through "hospitable": Louisa May Alcott, *The Journals,* 158.

"Gamp's Garrett" through ". . . a rainy day": Reisen, *Woman Behind* Little Women, 257.

"white and . . . flags flying": Louisa May Alcott, *The Journals,* 162.

"She is . . . hers do": Louisa May Alcott, *The Journals,* 163.

"Liberty is . . . many of us": Matteson, *Eden's Outcasts,* 330.

"He obviously wishes . . . your story": Reisen, *Woman Behind* Little Women, 265.

"I plod . . . my sisters": Louisa May Alcott, *The Journals,* 22.

"'Christmas won't . . . presents,' . . . the rug": Louisa May Alcott, *Little Women,* 1.

Epilogue

It reads better . . . the reason: Louisa May Alcott, *The Journals,* 166.

"Sent twelve . . ." through ". . . the need": Louisa May Alcott, *The Journals,* 166.

"The characters . . . simple facts": Louisa May Alcott, *Selected Letters,* 118.

"in the press . . . best critics": Louisa May Alcott, *Selected Letters,* 121.

"who the little . . ." through ". . . please anyone": Louisa May Alcott, *Little Women,* xix.

"literary spinster": Louisa May Alcott, *Selected Letters,* 125.

"paddle [her] own canoe": Louisa May Alcott, *The Journals,* 99.

"Publishers are . . . stupid style": Louisa May Alcott, *Selected Letters,* 122.

"the best and . . ." through ". . . Jo should marry": Louisa May Alcott, *Selected Letters,* 120.

"a funny match . . . vials of wrath": Louisa May Alcott, *Selected Letters,* 125.

"for stage . . . religious border": Reisen, *Woman Behind* Little Women, 2.

"a fervor . . . J.K. Rowling": Reisen, 1.

"People begin . . . a la Hawthorne": Reisen, 277.

"lion hunters": Shealy, *Alcott in Her Own Time,* ix.

"Driven to . . . in a week": Louisa May Alcott, *Selected Letters,* 128.

"known a startling . . . respectable traditions": Louisa May Alcott, *Unmasked,* 192–93.

"Father . . . wish I could": Cheever, *A Personal Biography,* 252.

Index